The
New Rules
of the Game

THE
NEW RULES
OF THE GAME

*The Four Key Experiences
Managers Must Have to Thrive
in the Non-Hierarchical 90s
and Beyond*

James R. Emshoff
with
Teri E. Denlinger

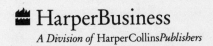

HarperBusiness
A Division of HarperCollinsPublishers

Library of Congress Cataloging-in-Publication Data

Emshoff, James R.
    The new rules of the game:the four key experiences managers
must have to thrive in the non-hierarchical 90s and beyond/
James R. Emshoff with Teri Denlinger.
      p. cm.
    Includes index.
    ISBN 0–88730–507–5
    1. Organizational change.   2. Organizational effectiveness.
3. Career development.   4. Middle managers.   I. Denlinger,
Teri,
1946– . II. Title.
HD58.8.E49 1991
658—dc20
                                91–6706
                                  CIP

Printed in the United States of America

91 92 93 94 CC/HC 7 6 5 4 3 2 1

To my daughter, Andrea,
whose views on what's important
are always insightful and often
inspirational to me.

Contents

Preface

When I first began to put my ideas and experiences together for this book in early 1989, I thought the fate of middle management careers would be a significant issue in the 1990s. As we go to press, I now believe it will be *the* single biggest issue of the decade.

I'm not saying this merely to hype the book. In fact, I wish I didn't have to make this prediction at all; but the factors that lead me to conclude that middle management careers are in trouble spell bad news for those managers and for the companies employing them.

What's changed since early 1989? Certainly not the fundamental supply-and-demand issues for middle managers that prompted me to write this book in the first place. The supply of very qualified middle managers will continue to expand through most of the 1990s, creating great competition for the slots that do open. At the same time, the corporate demand for traditional middle manager skills will continue to decrease; companies are looking for new types of skills to meet new types of business needs. When an excess of experienced middle management talent collides with a job environment in which skill requirements are changing, something has to give, and I guarantee it won't be the environment. As a middle manager, you cannot avoid dealing with this issue if you want to come out of the decade satisfied with your professional development. My book will help you come to grips with the new environment.

Now for the bad news about what's happening in the marketplace. I believe the middle management crisis will become the most serious issue of the decade because of the strategies that corporations are now adopting to restructure their organizations.

Frankly, I'm frightened by the way businesses are handling the pressure to change their management environments. Global competition and the threat of a severe recession at the beginning of the decade are motivating many companies to act on some of the tough decisions they might have been putting off. "Right-sizing" —eliminating unnecessary infrastructure and reducing management layers—is becoming the most common tactic of most corporations, and for the first time in history, they are starting with the white-collar rather than the blue-collar work force.

In most cases, right-sizing isn't part of a thoughtful strategy to redesign the whole corporate management structure and culture. Instead, it's an almost panicked reaction to pressures and problems, administered with the sheeplike justification that everyone else is doing the same thing. It is precisely this bandwagon phenomenon of right-sizing the management structure with no thought for the accompanying cultural changes that has me so concerned.

For middle managers, this bad news makes it that much more urgent that you actively create a professional development program, a career strategy, to ensure that you have the right credentials through the upcoming transition period of organizational change. Be assured that the ride will be bumpy and unpredictable. And don't expect anyone in your organization to take you by the hand and lead you around the land mines that have multiplied in the last 10 years. Based on my own experiences and on what other managers have told me, my book will help you devise a strategic battle plan by discussing and advising you on the four key experiences that all middle managers will need to have to advance and keep their positions in the 1990s: *people relationship skills, customer orientation, leadership,* and *risk-taking.* In the upcoming chapters, I offer an overview of the cultural changes we can expect, and discuss the four key experiences in great depth. I will also give you rules to follow and questions to ask that will help you audit your own company's strengths and weaknesses in these areas so that you can manage your way through these difficult times. Finally, I provide specific advice on managing many of your day-to-day career issues, as well as on executing your career strategy.

While my objective in writing this book is to help middle

managers through tough career decisions, I also offer a few suggestions to senior management readers. I sincerely wouldn't care to be 10–15 years younger and having to face the issues that today's middle managers are confronting, and I doubt that many of you would enjoy the prospect either. Like most of you, I have my own battle scars to show for how difficult life in the executive office is in today's corporate climate. But if the statistics can be believed, you have one important quality that your middle managers don't have—enthusiasm for your job and a commitment to your company.

Every survey I've seen, including the ones we completed every year at Diners Club, indicates that morale among middle managers is low, and still dropping. If you, as senior managers, respond to short-term economic pressures by taking short-term actions such as blowing out more of your middle management infrastructure, you are only exacerbating a problem that has already reached crisis proportions. You might not see the full impact for a while because of today's excess supply of managers. But what good are the bodies remaining in your middle management ranks if they lose loyalty and motivation with each downsizing they are lucky enough to miss?

I hope senior managers read this book as closely as middle managers do. But maintain your own perspective on the issues, and keep a few key questions in mind: Do you have a clear vision of how your management culture will change in the next three to five years to strengthen its overall competitive position in your industry? Can you tell your middle managers what skills and experiences they must develop to play a key role in your company as you go forward with these changes? What commitments are you prepared to make to generate long-term loyalty among your middle managers—or do you even want it? Tough questions, but I believe this book can help sharpen your answers. If you don't have final answers to important questions like these— and my sense is that most senior managers don't—your reactions to turbulent, short-term events, such as a recession, are likely to do a great deal of harm to an already volatile situation.

The stress that middle managers will experience in the next decade will be enormous, no matter what actions you take. But if middle management commitment and company loyalty continue to decline because senior executives do nothing to stop it, some unexpected and potentially devastating changes in our corporate culture could become permanent.

Even if the crisis in middle management careers does not become the top item of the decade, at the very least it will continue to be a major issue. The factors involved aren't abstract; we need to roll up our sleeves and concentrate our attention on creating the right solutions. Middle managers have no time to waste in building their plans of attack.

James R. Emshoff
Lake Forest, Illinois
January 31, 1991

Acknowledgments

It is easy to assign the first credit: to all the unnamed managers whose career events, small and large, have yielded the advice in this book.

Although I have drawn on experience from all phases of my career, the six years at Diners Club provided the richest and most relevant sources of material. As CEO of Diners Club, I had the ultimate responsibility of setting strategic directions and defining its overall management culture. Although some of my actions would have a short-term negative impact on our middle managers, my long-term goal was to create an environment that would be rewarding for all employees. I have tried to portray both the problems and the opportunities for middle managers that came with the culture change we implemented in Diners Club.

Not every managerial initiative undertaken by Diners Club is reported in this book; hundreds of others would have been equally relevant to the general issue of middle management careers in the 1990s. My special thanks go to all the Diners Club employees whose dedication and commitment to making the business successful drove the overall culture far more than anything else. My time at Diners Club will always be special because of that experience.

Even more data for this book came from interviews conducted with middle managers who had worked in various other companies during their careers, and some of their stories are used to illustrate specific points. Many were participants in the Executive MBA program at Northwestern University. I want to thank all of them for so generously sharing their time and experiences, helping to validate the basic structure used for career advice in general.

Teri Denlinger has been a true partner in the entire process of writing this book. I first met Teri when she interviewed me for an article on Diners Club in her former employer's internal management magazine. When I saw the article, I knew that Teri was especially skilled in understanding and communicating business culture in a way that really brings it to life. Teri has been my partner on this project from its inception. To the extent that the examples and discussions shape a clear, lasting mental picture, Teri's skills are the prime driver.

I received a great deal of support from the Citicorp organization, and am particularly grateful to Ira Rimerman, a member of Citicorp's Policy Committee, who endorsed the project from its inception and facilitated internal senior executive reviews of material from a publication policy standpoint. I also received a great deal of administrative and typing support from members of my staff at Diners Club. Among the people playing important roles in this regard were Juliette Cwiok, Donna Pagano, Sally Quilici, and Olga Turley.

A number of people played critical roles in helping to shape the structure and content of the material in the book. I would particularly like to acknowledge Mel Berger, vice president of William Morris Agency; Carol Franco, senior editor at Harvard Business School Press; and Cynthia Bates. The entire management team at Harper Business has been outstanding, but Virginia A. Smith, executive editor, went beyond any normal expectations in her dedication to creating a superior final product.

Finally, I want to thank my wife, Margie, and my daughter, Andrea. Just the challenge of my management role in Diners Club created working hours that heavily impinged on my family. When I debated starting this book project as an add-on activity, I got wholehearted support for it from both Margie and Andrea. They realized that most of my time to do the book would be stolen from normal family life, and for almost two years now, this book has changed our weekends, holidays, and vacations. After the fact, we have had some laughs about "Dad's book" getting wedged into the middle of different family activities. But my family's support of this project has been total, and without it, it would never have been completed. Thanks for the sacrifices.

The
New Rules
of the Game

1

The White-Collar Legacy

Every middle manager in corporate America is feeling the shock waves from the cultural upheaval taking place in today's business world. Corporations everywhere are altering their dimensions, struggling to get out from under the nonproductive bureaucracies that have left black holes in their organizations.

We're entering a decade of leaner, less bureaucratic structures that focus on empowerment, service, and the customer. Traditional organizational hierarchies are being junked in favor of flatter business units that bring a new dimension to employee-customer relationships. Downsizing and delayering are also important to the 1990s vision, and they're contributing to an entirely new—and definitely volatile—relationship between managers and companies, as well as to major changes in the definition of being a manager. While all these upheavals will vastly improve the management culture of tomorrow, right now they are inflicting heavy costs on the middle managers hardest hit by them.

The shift in our corporate structure is wreaking havoc with the careers of managers, and pink slips are being handed out at an alarming pace. In business's attempt to offset a sagging corporate economy, downsizing has spread like a plague in the middle management work force. Managers are having to deal with a brand-new set of parameters for doing business and getting ahead. It makes no difference if you administer the flow of paper or people; successful career paths in the 1980s for basically all

1

middle management positions have altered their course for the 1990s. Those of you who carefully plotted your careers to get from one point to the next are suddenly trapped in a maze of crumbling hierarchy and dwindling bureaucratic controls—with no way out.

You're not alone. The rapid change sweeping across our corporate environment is catching not only middle managers by surprise but also many U.S. and global businesses that simply aren't able to keep pace. Still, the middle manager is bearing the brunt of this cultural instability.

In today's American corporate culture, middle managers are the traditional bedrock within the managerial structure. You most directly control the policies and practices that move businesses forward from day to day, and you set the tone for how the hourly and nonexempt work force makes things happen. You are responsible for recruiting and training entry-level, frontline managers in the system. Perhaps even more critical, you represent the pool of talent from which the next generation of corporate executives will emerge.

Unfortunately, too many managers fall short on delivering the right credentials and experience for the 1990s. Mine isn't the only executive office with stacks of unsolicited letters and résumés intended to introduce a manager and present skills that might be relevant to our company. Headhunters tell me they're also inundated with people, good people, putting the best spin on "what I've done in the last 10 years," but nothing stands out. Their résumés reek of accomplishments that worked in the past but which fail to touch the hot buttons of the 1990s.

Take a hard look at your own career. Do your skills meet the needs of a culture that turns the traditional way of doing business inside out? Ask yourself whether your résumé reflects an ability to lead and motivate people in an empowered environment. Can you directly make a difference when you respond to customer needs and demands? What about your judgment in assessing and taking risks, your ability to view and lead the business from an entrepreneurial perspective, or your competence in developing people relationships to move the business forward? These are qualities that the emerging culture will increasingly demand of middle managers.

Many of you view your future as an enigma; you're uncertain about how best to capitalize on job opportunities that could help you achieve your professional goals. For some of you, the situation is fast becoming critical; you sense that control of your career is quickly vanishing and that there are real threats to your ability to maintain any position at all, even as a middle manager.

There are no easy remedies to the management crisis. The cultural changes inflicting so much pain and uncertainty on the middle management ranks are diverse and have spread quickly. I guarantee that in the next decade you'll confront some of the threats to your career described in this book.

A Matter of Supply

One of the most visible causes of your career puzzle is sheer supply of talent. We're creating the largest and most qualified pool of managers this country has ever had to take on the challenges of corporate leadership—so large, in fact, that for every one of you who falters, there are several managers ready to take your place.

Traditionally, people aged 35 to 45 have been the primary source of middle management talent. The baby boomers have created a one-time explosion in the supply of individuals competing for jobs. In 1980 there were 25.6 million 35–45-year-olds, representing 11.4 percent of the country's total population. In 1990 this age group had increased to 35.4 million people, constituting 14.4 percent of our population. By the year 2000 they will number 43.9 million, or 16.4 percent of the population. The demographic message is clear: This generation of potential leaders will need to compete more intensely for open positions throughout their lives simply because the system doesn't expand to fit the one-time bubble of baby boomers moving through the ranks.

Another strain on management careers stems from today's middle managers being the most educationally qualified ever to occupy such positions in American corporate history. In 1980, 95,000 people aged 35–45 held MBAs. That number increased to 365,000 during 1990 and is expected to jump to more than

665,000 by the year 2000. Having invested so much to acquire this degree, managers have a legitimate expectation that it will benefit their careers. But today the MBA is increasingly viewed as necessary just to stay even. In other words, the corporate culture of tomorrow will be based on a rapid expansion in supply of managers with greater credentials for the available jobs.

Shrinking Demand Following Corporate Downsizing

The expanded supply of managerial talent represents only one side of the story. The other side is what we politely refer to as "downsizing." This euphemism for firing employees emphasizes that they didn't necessarily do a poor job—they were merely too expensive to maintain as part of the work force. From January to October 1990, 170,000 white-collar workers were out of jobs, and new layoffs were being reported at twice the rate as that for the previous year. A handsome early retirement or severance package used to accompany such action, but these payments are being trimmed. According to an article in *Business Week* (Oct. 1, 1990), such offerings averaged 22 weeks in duration in 1989 but shrank to 18 weeks for 1990 (through October). It looks as if the only people doing any hiring these days are outplacement firms.

A downsizing decision in highly visible companies such as AT&T and General Electric gets substantial publicity. Between 1982 and 1988 Mobil reduced its white-collar payroll by 17 percent, and DuPont by 15 percent. Ford trimmed its worldwide salary ranks in 35 of 36 quarters over a nine-year period between 1979 and 1988. But downsizing isn't restricted to a few large companies. An industry-wide survey conducted by the American Management Association (AMA) in late 1988 confirmed the ramifications of the management reduction process. Thirty-five percent of the respondents downsized between mid-1987 and mid-1988, eliminating more than 10 percent of their work force. Almost 15 percent planned to downsize the following year, placing 10 percent of their employees at risk.

The facts are irrefutable. Any growth in jobs in the next decade will not come from our traditionally large corporate base. Since 1980, Fortune 500 companies have reduced their employment base by 2.8 million, and the ripple effect of this restructuring has been an additional loss of more than six million jobs in other companies.

It wasn't always this way. Between 1983 and 1989, white-collar numbers increased by 29 percent, while the blue-collar force decreased. Today that situation is completely reversed, for not terribly complicated reasons. Think about it. Cutting out blue-collar workers by the droves eventually became easy. After corporations got the hang of it, they realized that even better financial gains were to be had by eliminating the higher paid, starched white collars. Long-term strategies and goals weren't the driving force for these actions. They were motivated by the need to survive, pure and simple.

With all the corporate shuffling and restructuring, where are new jobs being created now? Primarily in smaller companies in the service industries. Nearly 20 million jobs were created by entrepreneurs between 1970 and 1980. One forecast is that by the year 2000, 85 percent of the work force will be employed in firms with fewer than 100 people. This kind of company usually has not employed many middle managers. It's no wonder that delay-ering and downsizing have intensified the career path concerns of middle managers when most of the growth is occurring in areas that apparently do not need their talents.

The Loyalty Factor

While some companies try to support the needs of laid-off employees through counseling, outplacement programs, or job placement, many companies simply aren't prepared for the emotional turmoil that comes with downsizing. Morale and productivity issues monopolize executive meetings, but few solutions are being brought to the table.

Take a look at the guy in the office next to yours. He probably won't be around in five years. What about that strategic long-range plan you and your team developed? How many on your team will play out their roles all the way to the end?

The manager who planned on retiring from the company she joined from school is long gone. And the statistics aren't very encouraging for a move in a different direction. An estimated three million managers got their pink slips in the past decade as companies, trying to offset the Japanese invasion, stepped up cost-cutting measures. A recent *Industry Week* (Jan. 8, 1990) survey that drew responses from 507 managers below the rank of CEO and president reported that only 49 percent are fairly confident they'll be with their current employer five years from now. In response to the same question in 1970, three-quarters of the middle managers planned on being with their employers five years later. The number dropped to 70 percent in 1976, to 64 percent in 1979, and to 58 percent in 1983. This sentiment—which continues to increase—does not say much for company loyalty.

Asked to compare their current attitudes with how they felt two years before, 42 percent said they're more likely now to actively pursue outside employment opportunities. Six years before, the same *Industry Week* survey discovered that only 36 percent of the respondents held this view. Although 56 percent believe they're being given opportunities to develop skills and experience leading to a higher position, 42 percent say they are not. Even provided with training and skills for upward mobility, 45 percent say their chances for advancement are poor at best.

It's disconcerting that even during economic good times, management attitudes have soured to this extent. But leveraged buyouts, corporate raiders, downsizing, and a host of other factors have made it clear that if you don't take care of yourself, no one else will. Even the dedicated professional whose work ethic is unchallenged often feels the most betrayed and vies to be first in line at the exit. Corporate loyalty is rapidly becoming a thing of the past.

What You Know Versus What You Need to Know

New rules for successful entry into executive management slots are being permanently changed, making career decisions a white-knuckles experience for middle managers. Downsizing is only one important issue. Skills and career steps that once ensured entry into senior management might be totally wrong for today. While all the MBAs, the financial gurus, and the marketing geniuses are playing "gotcha" games on their way up the corporate ladder, the culture as they know it today is being swept out from under them.

Middle managers are beginning to feel like ingredients in a large corporate stew—flavored with equal amounts of both the traditional and the emerging culture. Executive chefs mix them into recipes for a 1980s management product on some occasions, and into 1990s recipes on others. It's a combination that can't be found in any popular cookbook. If managers don't fit the management product of the moment, they're dissolved and replaced by a fresh recruit from an endless supply of ingredients. Scary? Yes. And very real.

Going Forward

For many middle managers, just coping with the career implications of the supply-and-demand conditions is difficult enough. But these conditions, combined with the dramatic changes in career advancement game rules, have more and more middle managers retreating to a survival mentality. They concede any chance for executive promotion and prefer to shut their eyes, hoping the issue will go away. Their actions assume that such changes haven't occurred.

This is no solution. If you're a middle manager bent on keeping your eyes wide open, you won't view the new rules as another uncontrollable threat. Instead, you'll recognize that different rules provide an opportunity for you to differentiate yourself from the middle management clutter. If you understand where management philosophies are headed, you also recognize your need to develop and position your career so that you can break away from the pack.

Any chance of a successful career in the next decade depends on your ability to envision the emerging management culture, as well as to develop the necessary skills to succeed in that culture. Without this vision, you won't be able to capitalize on the challenges the new culture creates. You also need to be prepared to develop a strategy and skills that fit both the traditional and emerging management cultures. Keep in mind, however, that certain skills may be demanded of managers in areas that are not obvious now but will become evident as the new management culture unfolds.

Make no mistake about this new career path process: it has clear risks. Managing your career through the transition between two corporate cultures requires that you walk a fine line. Don't wait until the emerging trends are obvious before learning new skills and acquiring experience more attuned to the 1990s culture. Otherwise, you'll be lost in the supply of endlessly qualified managers. On the other hand, if you move too far ahead of today's managerial philosophies, your career can become derailed before you have a chance to use any of your developing capabilities.

If you feel as if you're walking a balance beam, you are. Falling off takes only one wrong move, and you may not be able to climb back on. For managers to succeed, they must strategically position themselves to work comfortably within the boundaries of this cultural metamorphosis.

Take Control of Your Future

You can't ignore the impact or pace of the changing dynamics within corporate America. Individual weather fronts sweeping across a geographic area do not fundamentally alter the landscape, but numerous fronts converging on one area often leave vast changes behind. The low-pressure system over corporate America for the past decade isn't about to pass over without a thunderstorm or two. So do you take precautions or get drenched? Frankly, there's not much protection available today for the soggy manager who leaves his or her raincoat hanging in the closet. To help you answer many of your career questions, I describe in my book four key experiences that you will need to evaluate, practice, and master in your own career. I've drawn on my own experiences that are most likely to parallel situations you've encountered or will encounter in the future. These key experiences will not only be required of all middle managers in the 1990s but are also instructive to senior executives who are restructuring their organizations as they struggle with an outmoded and unprepared work force.

Managing people relationships, customer orientation, leadership, and *risk-taking* are the prerequisite experiences in managing your career through the 1990s.

My intent is to help you not only in avoiding the cultural traps that are snaring middle managers but also in capitalizing on career opportunities. I've been fortunate to have had a variety of professional experiences that are particularly relevant to the issues middle managers face today. My objective is to make my experiences pay off for you. Many of my own war stories exemplify the lessons that highlight situations you'll want to avoid at all costs and point to preventive measures you can apply to your own career decisions.

While many of the techniques for moving from the traditional culture into the emerging one haven't been discovered, there will be substantial rewards for the players who best interpret the clues and execute their plan for managing through the transition. Those who expect to master the new cultural dynamics will need to solve the riddle: How do you successfully advance from the traditional management structure into the emerging culture of the 1990s and beyond?

Let's get started on the answers.

2

The Forces of Change in the Emerging Culture of the 1990s

Talk to just about any middle manager today and you'll hear horror stories—about layoffs, companies going under, corporations and entire industries undergoing massive change, career paths being derailed, and managers facing months of unemployment. It is hard to glean from any one cultural change a prescription for new career tactics for managers. But collectively, cultural changes have prompted permanent changes in the managerial structures and processes of the 1990s.

The trouble is, before managers even begin to recover from one force of change, they're being pushed by another. If *change* is the buzzword for the 1990s, the pace of change is like a swarm of bees hovering over American corporations. And middle managers have been the first to get stung.

To use cultural changes to your professional advantage, you must first understand the fundamental forces driving them. I believe that there are five forces responsible for changing the way business is conducted. These forces will have a significant impact on your career for years to come and will define the issues that corporations must address and the demands that they will place on their managers.

Service Industry Focus

The first force to be understood is this country's move away from its historical focus on manufacturing industries to a new focus on services. During the 1980s, the United States took a giant step toward becoming an economy dominated by the service industry. If anything, this trend is expected to accelerate throughout the 1990s. The shift to a service economy brings up many managerial issues, including issues of organization, since the key factors for running successful service businesses generally are quite different from those for manufacturing industries.

In most manufacturing environments, competitive product differences are easy to define but difficult to overcome. Patent positions are an extreme example of product protection barriers; technical knowledge, supplier relationships, and a host of other factors can also create such barriers in the marketplace. As a result, a manufacturing company's success is often perceived to be more dependent on the company's production process than on the products themselves.

I have seen how overconcentrating on production processes entrapped my former employer, Campbell Soup. Campbell's expertise and commitment to canned-food products have made it the third-largest can manufacturer in the United States, demonstrating the company's size and reliance on this form of packaging. Some years ago, Campbell realized that dry-food technology would play an increasing role in U.S. eating habits. Not surprisingly, the company's interest in pursuing the dry-soup market intensified, and eventually it formulated a dry-soup product superior to anything else on the market. It failed, however, to achieve any significant market share.

Looking at the situation today, I don't think there's anything too mystifying about consumers' lack of enthusiasm over the product. How would you feel about purchasing dry soup packaged in a can? Probably the same as most consumers felt when Campbell launched the product. The company insisted on retaining its traditional packaging form, and its technological edge in the packaging industry almost, but not quite, carried the product.

But it was not until many years after this setback that Campbell was willing to make another serious effort to penetrate the dry-soup market—this time using packaging dictated by consumer preferences.

Few companies in the service industry have any natural barriers comparable to ones like this. Services are generally easy to duplicate, and the barriers of competitive entry are low. As a result, *how* services are delivered is secondary to *what* services are delivered. If a service company fails to satisfy a customer, a competitor generally will be there to provide something that hits the bull's-eye.

As the U.S. economy moves toward service-dominated structures, management structures and processes will also become increasingly service-driven. This has tremendous implications for keeping up with customer needs and organizing rapid responses to those needs. The manufacturing-oriented processes simply aren't sufficient to succeed in this new environment.

For instance, during the 1980s almost every major food-processing company tried to enter the restaurant business. Superficially, this extension certainly looked logical: as food consumption at home declined, it seemed reasonable to assume that food consumption in restaurants would increase. The opportunities seemed endless for the food processors, but they never materialized.

The theoretical benefits of transferring food-processing management know-how into restaurant businesses failed in execution for virtually every food processor during the 1980s—and almost always for the same reasons. The pace of change in the restaurant marketplace, dictated by shifting interest in restaurant themes and food products, was simply too fast for the food-processing decision-makers. Restaurants operated by food-processing businesses couldn't compete with those owned and managed by organizations with a pure service culture. The management systems simply weren't compatible.

Over time, some manufacturing companies have begun to integrate the new service orientation—aimed at listening and responding more intently to customer preferences—into their management processes. I witnessed this evolution while heading the Beverage Business Unit for Campbell Soup. You might assume that if any company is driven by consumer preferences, it ought to be the consumer packaged-goods manufacturer. Not so. I quickly had to come to grips with the issue of customer preference when dealing with Campbell's way of making product formulation decisions.

We were in the middle of a major project to develop a new line of kids' beverages. Funny thing about kids—they always know exactly what they like. Funny thing, too, about adults—we presume to know better. We fell into this trap at Campbell.

Campbell had a long tradition of actively involving senior managers in the taste evaluations of its food products that took place before a new product was introduced into test markets. Management comments from these sessions were used by the food technicians to adjust or reformulate flavors and other essential characteristics. An ongoing concern of mine was just how far we should take product formulation based on management rather than consumer feedback. Taste is obviously subjective. Could a group of 50-year-old executives effectively judge what a 5-year-old would want to drink?

To answer that question, we developed a market research study in which preschool and elementary school children judged our various test beverages. To validate the results, we even repeated the same test formulation on different days and compared the ratings. To everyone's amazement, the tests were incredibly accurate—more precise, in fact, than those conducted with management.

Accuracy is one thing, but the real issue was preference, and the facts spoke for themselves. There was no correlation between the kids' beverage preferences and those management had expressed on their behalf. As a result, we scrapped the senior management taste sessions.

This lesson and others like it are being learned by corporations seeking to build their customer relationships. Gordon McGovern, then CEO of Campbell Soup, quickly endorsed our new procedure for beverage testing. One of the food industry's strongest advocates for greater use of customer response data in designing new products, he even launched a small restaurant so that he could get consumer feedback on some of his preliminary product formulations.

McGovern believed the most conclusive evidence of product quality was seeing an empty plate returned to the kitchen instead of a half-eaten plate of food. Restaurant owners are regularly privy to that feedback, but unfortunately, not many manufacturing executives see the same need for regular customer feedback on product performance.

The danger in any business is managers believing they are clairvoyant about the customer's needs and preferences. While management may well develop a sixth sense about customer preferences, relying solely on such input is risky. Today companies are beginning to recognize this risk as they make more of an effort to take business actions based on customer feedback.

Ask yourself how your company is responding to pressures to become more customer-oriented. More important, how do you fit into that picture? Make sure you're properly positioned for new managerial priorities focused on customers before waiting for someone to spell it out for you. Otherwise, you won't be part of the outcome.

As the forces of change continue to drive the United States toward a service economy, management processes across all industries will be overhauled to provide customer information about company offerings and to create faster responses to customer queries or problems.

Nonproductive Management Infrastructure

The cause of corporate infrastructure growth during the 1980s isn't easy to diagnose. Indeed, much of the infrastructure put in place reflected some of the successful management patterns identified by Tom Peters and Bob Waterman in their seminal book *In Search of Excellence: Lessons from America's Best-Run Companies* (1982). Their model involves decentralized business management units with an overlay of centralized controls—what the authors call "loose/tight management."

The philosophy behind this model is to give individual businesses within the corporation the freedom to do things that promote growth; that freedom is then counterbalanced by tight, centralized controls, largely financially driven. This system worked well through the early 1980s, but many companies haven't been able to maintain the balance. The growth of centralized control staffs outstripped the growth of the smaller business units.

The imbalance was magnified by the presence of an ever-expanding army of MBAs in central control positions. Their energies were concentrated on preventing mistakes and asking penetrating questions. The notion that their jobs were to promote innovation and growth was a fallacy. And who could blame them for their focus? They got positive reinforcement from corporate officers who received stacks of computer analyses to support questions during business review meetings. But attitudes about central staff infrastructures changed dramatically as the decade drew to a close. The downsizing and delayering decisions that struck terror in the hearts of middle managers largely occurred in staff areas not directly supporting business activities.

There's plenty of room for further restructuring in the eyes of many corporate executives, but such change won't come easily. It can be unnerving to remove an infrastructure that a company has taken years to build. When control no longer flows upward, CEOs lose their comfort zones, their own control systems. Still, the onset of change will force CEOs and the remaining corporate administrative infrastructure to disassemble this structural control themselves. Following hard examination of the facts, many corporate leaders have already concluded that they have made huge investments in infrastructure that is not contributing to the efficiency or effectiveness of basic business unit performance. These investments are the first to go in downsizing actions.

You might wonder how infrastructure investments can get so out of balance in so many organizations. Part of the answer lies in the enthusiastic reception of new information-processing technologies and graphics packages. Senior management simply overdosed on these products, and the middle managers who produced them capitalized on that enthusiasm by increasing staff. But there's a more fundamental issue at work here.

Left unchecked, staff bureaucracies will self-perpetuate as long as the organization fails to tie employee performance to core business performance—that is, the generation of more revenues for products and services delivered to customers *or* the improvement of cost efficiency in delivering those products and services. Once employees are no longer subject to customer-based measures of organizational effectiveness, the controls on bureaucratic growth rapidly dissipate and expansion becomes a self-fulfilling prophecy.

Public-sector organizations often are criticized for being the extreme in bureaucratic complexity. I believe this perception is correct. Public-sector bureaucracies grow dizzyingly complex because they can't link the actions of their employees to the customer through revenue as the fundamental measure of success. When I consulted for the U.S. Navy, I got a firsthand taste of how bureaucracy can grow within public-sector organizations. In all my consulting days, the Navy was by far the most complex, entangled organization I've ever encountered.

My assignment was to apply private-sector planning processes to the Naval Air System Command, which was responsible for designing, developing, and purchasing all Navy aircraft. After three years of steadily banging my head against the Navy hierarchy, I can say the effort was a categorical failure.

The operating system of the Navy is so intricate that it's virtually impossible for anyone to have a real sense of what's going on. I soon realized that the confusion is a perfectly rational consequence of the grade-level structure for civil servants. One of the most common justifications for upgrading a job to a higher grade level is the increase in funding dollars that flow through the job as part of an approval or control process. The critical phrase here is "flow through." The entire Navy organization wins when money passes through as many management hands as possible on its path from congressional appropriations to the production of air systems products. I observed some of the most unbelievably convoluted steps being taken to ensure that everyone "touched" the money. Try to interrupt this stream and you found that you were taking on the entire U.S. Navy.

Another structural detail that thwarted our planning efforts was the coexistence in one organization of a military and a civilian culture. On three-year assignments, military officers had little time to make their mark in the organization. Since civilians typically were long-term employees, officers depended a great deal on civilians' knowledge of the organization to help them leave their mark. This interaction could have produced a cooperative working relationship, but it seldom did.

With an influx of new officers every three years, it was unlikely that the two groups would develop a workable chemistry for making positive change. So civilians resisted any change. They weren't indifferent or reactionary; they simply recognized that time restrictions alone would never permit any real change to occur.

Compared to other public-sector organizations, the structure in the Naval Air System Command was neither unusual nor particularly complicated. The system produced extremely rational behavior on the part of individuals who had to operate within it. It merely took time and patience for an outsider to understand the reasoning behind the behavior. But the issue is not whether there is a rational reason for the growth of the bureaucracy—it is whether the structure is efficient and effective. On that score, the system was a disaster.

In the middle of my consulting assignment for the Navy, I began to wonder how the organization could survive, much less flourish, over time. Then I realized the normal customer control processes didn't exist in this situation. For example, as long as the Navy's aircraft got built, no one was going to challenge the Navy's means of doing this. It's nearly impossible to say who could have put a stop to the inefficiency and nonproductiveness created by the bureaucratic structure. I couldn't find a soul in or outside the Navy able to do so.

Perhaps the most important foundation of the private-sector system is customers having a choice of purchases. The theory is that those organizations that don't meet marketplace demands for quality and price either restructure or go away. If you want reality, however, look at your own organization, or at any business with corporate layers that aren't customer-related. How many layers have no relationship whatsoever to your customer base? Is your organization any different from the Navy? I doubt it.

Nonproductive managerial infrastructures, however, are finally being forced to change. Senior executives are feeling more confident about making changes that have already proven successful in some corporations. Since human nature dictates that risk-takers find safety in numbers, the level of management confidence in these moves continues to grow with each new announcement of another company's effort to eliminate irrelevant layers of infrastructure. The first back-to-basics cuts have been made in almost every organization. Chances are you have been spared so far. But each round of downsizing increases the odds that you'll be in the next group.

Where is the safe harbor to weather the storm? I don't think you'll find it if you wait to start the search once the waves have already begun to wash over your desk. Take the initiative before you're threatened. Make an objective assessment of your *real* contributions to your company's customer relationships. The more indirect your link to customers, the more vulnerable you are. Sooner or later you'll find yourself at risk, and you probably won't have anything like the federal government bureaucracy to protect you.

Your only protection is in repositioning your role so that you contribute to the core of the business. That could take time and calculated career actions, but the elimination of nonproductive infrastructure won't stop soon.

Global Business Structures

One of the significant forces of change over the past decade has been the evolution of the global business complex that interconnects markets. Suppliers and competitors in various markets are also more interconnected. For example, although Chrysler continues to publicly wave the American flag in its advertising campaigns, the company's products are hybrids created and produced in worldwide locations. Today there is virtually no aspect of an organization's product creation and distribution that doesn't have global implications.

The shift to the global business structure during the 1980s made many U.S. companies that chose to concentrate only on the domestic market extremely vulnerable. Their strategy of vertical integration gave them marketplace domination, but they are now beginning to see the pitfalls of such a strategy.

In reality, vertical integration can thwart innovation in businesses linked by common ownership. Because no single competitor owns the vertically integrated position, an organization can establish the economic pattern and speed of technological innovation. Chief executives often resist new technologies because capital writeoffs are required before full depreciation of assets occurs. Without the driving force of other competition, an organization gets a false sense of being insulated against the competition. Only when foreign competitors enter the marketplace with different, superior, and cheaper products does the vulnerability of the vertically integrated organization become truly apparent. It's happening today in many U.S. industries.

The auto industry offers the most striking example. During the 1970s Detroit flexed its muscles and demanded that the answer to the pollution crisis be one that would minimize the need to alter its production systems or engineering designs. I give you the catalytic converter, an ugly device at home on your car's exhaust system. The converter's job is to burn pollutants from behind the fuel-inefficient engines that created the need for them in the first place. Everyone in the United States who owns a car with a catalytic converter would, no doubt, trade the system in for a pack of bubble gum. They crack, gurgle, and stink.

Japanese automakers went about solving the pollution dilemma another way. They recognized that breeding pollutants and then attempting to burn them off might not be the most productive remedy for polluted air. Although the Japanese ultimately depended on the catalytic converter, they first designed a more efficient engine that eliminated many of the pollutants from the start. But this took time, a requirement Detroit wasn't willing to tolerate. The Japanese were willing to make the investment and subsequently got better results for their persistence.

The global business structure is destined to alter corporate America. Vertical integration strategies will undoubtedly become less popular, and supplier relationships will be developed globally. Companies will be forced to make hard decisions about where their real technical expertise lies. They may find that many of the business units in their vertically integrated chain are simply a drag on corporate initiatives. Painful readjustments are likely to be made as a result.

In the end, corporations will have no choice but to reevaluate and streamline their product offerings to compete in the global marketplace. Global competition is already here and shows no signs of disappearing. Your role as a middle manager depends on your ability to adapt yourself and your skills to this changing environment. You have to be able to apply a keen knowledge of the global market while keeping up with local idiosyncrasies. Globalization is big business, and if you want to stick around to see just how big, your focus for career advancement will have to include an ability to think globally.

Business as Real Estate

We've witnessed tremendous upheaval in the ownership of corporate America. Even companies that haven't changed ownership have experienced great change in the relationship between equity and debt that finance their growth. Just turn on the radio or pick up today's paper. Junk bonds and LBOs have dramatically affected the strategic thinking of every CEO.

Any corporation on the New York Stock Exchange is a target for a takeover run if the price is right. Who would have guessed 10 years ago that Sears would protect itself against a buyout through a plan to sell its corporate headquarters? Who would have thought that a company as large as R.J. Reynolds would disappear from public ownership, and that debt payment would become the top concern of its new corporate senior management team?

The CEO of a multibusiness corporation must work very carefully to ensure that the value of each business is reflected in the market value of the corporation as a whole. If the equation doesn't add up, the CEO had better worry.

Not long ago, the benefits of synergy were generally accepted. It was thought that individual businesses operating under a compatible, strategic umbrella were worth more as a whole than as separate entities. Marketplace values today, however, don't always reflect the benefits of synergy. When this occurs, corporate raiders are ready to strike.

Richard Ferris, former CEO of the now defunct Allegis Corporation, bought into the concept of synergy. Allegis assets consisted primarily of United Airlines, Hertz Rent-A-Car, Westin Hotels, and Hilton International Hotels. Ferris wanted to create an umbrella corporation to bring components of the travel industry into one cohesive unit to more efficiently serve customers. His idea seemed to be sound. Allegis seemed to be worth more as a whole than as a combination of its individual units.

But announcing the synergy strategy made the market price for Allegis stock, for reasons still not completely understood, fall below the breakup value of the individual business components. Ferris never had a chance. Raiders, recognizing that the company was undervalued, invaded, took control, sold off the pieces, and then made their killing.

Allegis wasn't the only casualty in the 1980s. Large conglomerates have been easy prey. They're constantly monitored by raiders, forcing the CEO to function as a kind of real estate broker. CEOs must carve, sell, and shape chunks of the organization just to retain their jobs and keep the business alive.

CEOs have come to recognize that the individual companies under a corporate umbrella must be organized to operate on a stand-alone basis. Otherwise, flexibility in buying and selling units simply doesn't exist. Without such flexibility, the CEO—and his or her company—becomes a vulnerable target. Ownership options have also multiplied with the forces of change. LBOs, Employee Stock Ownership Plans (ESOPs), and other measures of ownership that create new bonds between managers and owners are taking shape, altering management attitudes and practices.

The uncertainties created by these cultural shifts make it tough for middle managers who are groping for some sense of personal stability and professional growth. And they don't see the emerging culture as one that offers much of either. The additional debt load many companies have been forced to assume to create competitive returns for shareholders has forced managers to react at the first hint of bad financial news. The stable environment in which companies could hang tough through a weak sales situation has been replaced by "do something to fix it" demands on managers.

Rather than being protected by a corporate complex—shielded from the ultimate performance problems unless the whole company goes bankrupt—middle managers are finding their individual business units being treated more like independent companies. The risk of your unit being sold or wound down for poor performance is real, and a job for you is not likely to automatically appear somewhere else in the parent corporation if that happens. Those of you who enjoy working in a smaller, more entrepreneurial environment will find more opportunity to work in such an environment in the future. But you'd better manage your job changes carefully—even within your parent company—or you could be surprised at the outcome.

Attention to Management Process

The 1980s was a boom time for authors providing advice to managers. A deluge of literary management directives introduced corporate executives to the emerging culture. Peters and Waterman's *In Search of Excellence* remains the most discussed analysis of management processes. Sales were estimated to have exceeded 4 million copies worldwide in the first four years of publication. Other books followed, demonstrating a newfound market for literature assisting executives with making key decisions on running their companies. As of 1989, U.S. sales of business books were averaging approximately 1.5 million copies each year. The growth of the executive literary market in the 1980s demonstrates that management was seriously interested in principles for redesigning organizations and processes.

Increasing publicity about successful management process and structure made some companies into role models that set new standards of performance and excellence. The management patterns of these companies are becoming quite clear, and corporate executives are looking for management talent that can help them restructure their businesses into similar formats. What can we learn from these model companies about the patterns in which you'll need to fit?

They are businesses that combat hierarchy and bureaucratic controls. They are value-driven, and they use service relationships with their customers as the catalyst for fine-tuning internal and external functions. Their employees don't get rewards for writing reports; they get rewards for taking action. Model companies think big and act small. Communication is relentlessly informal. The organization maximizes strengths, minimizes weaknesses, and treats all employees with dignity. Thus, extraordinary results are obtained from ordinary people. A healthy tolerance for failure keeps innovation alive and flourishing.

The effort to create an entrepreneurial culture at every level within an organization encourages people to roll up their sleeves, dig in, and take the initiatives they would if they owned the business themselves. The goal is to convert professionally objective, functional managers into entrepreneurs who are motivated to make a real difference for the business.

Despite the fact that many senior executives read the publications on the various theories about management style, few believe they'll find a cookbook with just the right recipes for organizing and operating a large company. But the abundance of information has forced senior management to focus more closely on management process and organizational structure. Considering the speed of change and what we know about it, they're not likely to relax that focus anytime soon. This will put even more pressure on middle managers.

Does your résumé show that you have broken away from the traditional culture and into the emerging one? For instance, have you identified customer expectations and prompted your business to act on your findings? What have you done to unleash the potential contributions others in your organization can make? Can you honestly say you work to eliminate bureaucracy, or are you sometimes the cause of it? Are you functional and territorial as a manager, or are your actions on the cutting edge of entrepreneurialism? Increasingly, your value as a professional will be measured along these lines.

Responding to Change

The importance of the five forces of change—service industry focus, nonproductive management infrastructure, global business structures, businesses as real estate, and attention to management process—won't diminish with time. I selected them precisely because there is little doubt that each has already had a significant impact on the management culture of corporate America. What is only now beginning to come clear, however, is how these forces are working together to accelerate the restructuring of the American corporate culture in the 1990s.

Up to now, most companies have reacted to these forces with narrowly defined solutions to the individual issues involved. Senior managers have maintained a problem-solving mentality; that is, they seek the tried-and-true solutions that other companies have used for the same problems. For example, faced with shrinking margins and earnings declines, the immediate reaction of many senior executives has been to delayer: to attack the bureaucracy and remove layers of corporate staff. Similarly, the new religion on product quality has produced the predictable corporate response that employees and customers must be convinced of the company commitment to deliver "nothing but the best." Company slogans, executive speeches, and incentive programs follow a strikingly similar pattern across companies that get the quality bug.

But these fragmented attacks on the problems haven't worked. Corporate executives are discovering that narrowly focusing on a few aspects of the forces of change provides only temporary relief. The corporate organization cannot be neatly compartmentalized, with specific issues managed separately and independently. Even when problems appear to be standard across an industry, senior managers are discovering that the solutions required for their company's problems aren't necessarily those that work in another company's corporate culture. To assume that ready-made solutions always work is equivalent to trying to fit a Chevy transmission into a Ford and expecting it to work. Senior managers are also finding that the conventional wisdom on solutions doesn't even produce the promised short-term results.

Over the next decade, we'll see senior management deal with all the forces of change as a complex of interacting problems. Instead of knee-jerk programs to cut bureaucracy because profit margins are squeezed, we're likely to see thoughtful reorganization plans to make the corporation and its businesses fundamentally more competitive in their markets. These plans will certainly deal with issues of cost efficiency; but they will also focus on business decentralization to capitalize on opportunities for equity compensation as an employee motivational tool. The plans also will address globalization by facilitating global partnerships and supplier relationships that were simply too complex to administer through the giant corporate structures of the past.

The new service culture will undoubtedly continue to fuel corporate efforts to attain greater customer focus and product quality. But the quality ritual we have seen until now will be replaced by a total rethink of business strategy and mechanisms for delivering value. Solutions to quality problems will incorporate issues of organizational structure, employee motivation systems, and soul-searching redefinitions of the business, its customers, suppliers, and competitors. This response will be a far cry from slapping a catchy quality slogan on bulletin boards. Rather than simply advertising their awareness of quality issues, companies will have to demonstrate it daily to their customers.

These changes will modify the charter of corporate leaders. Previously, too many executives have been comfortable filling no more than a watchdog role, ensuring that management didn't make any major errors. In the future senior executives must take charge of the forces of change by actively designing the right corporate culture and making the necessary adaptations in strategy. These leaders will need to establish environments that challenge their managerial teams to perform in ways that can't be dictated through the policy manual.

Corporate Commitments to Pioneer Change

A number of innovative companies have already adopted standards for change that will become commonplace in the 1990s. Typically, they do so either when they find themselves at a crossroads where doing things a little better each year doesn't cut it, or when the chief has a fire in his or her belly to take the risks that will make the company world-class.

Perhaps the most visible pioneer is General Electric. When Jack Welch took over as chairman and CEO in 1981, he took as his mandate the redefinition of GE's empire. No U.S. company has a broader stake in the U.S. economy than GE, and no one saw more clearly than Jack Welch that GE had to be totally restructured to be competitive. Welch made the commitment to change GE before its foundational strength was so sapped that its leadership position would be threatened.

As Welch ripped apart the existing GE culture and implemented his bold vision, the media watched and reported. At one point, the press referred to Welch as "Neutron Jack": when the Welch bomb detonated in a GE business unit, the buildings were left intact but the people disappeared. The name stuck, as did many unflattering stories about the transition, but Welch persevered with his vision.

GE underwent major surgery to unload its bureaucracy, leaving the fewest possible layers between management and the employees who deal with its customers. Welch worked to flatten and broaden the structure to allow employees the freedom to make their own decisions. He expected GE's low-level managers to act as entrepreneurs in their business areas.

By the end of the 1980s, Welch was being lauded as the American global leader of the 1990s for his successful transformation of GE. There are many fascinating articles about the Welch philosophy and his method of implementing changes. I suggest you get your hands on these articles; Welch's brand of restructuring could well be one your company will undergo.

According to Welch, words like *downsizing, reducing,* and *cutting,* often used to describe the company's restructuring, completely miss the point. Instead, he views his task as *liberating, facilitating,* and *unleashing* the energy and initiative of GE's people.

While his vision is frightening to managers caught in traditional cultures, Welch's changes are likely to become standard philosophy. A bellwether of change in corporate America, GE is bound to find many followers as other corporations realize how they must operate to meet the new challenges.

Jan Carlzon's turnaround of SAS Airlines is another example of bold maneuvering. When he took over SAS in 1981, Carlzon faced a more urgent challenge than Welch did. The company was about to lose over $20 million that year and was threatened with either going bankrupt or being swallowed up by one of its global competitors. With little choice but to take aggressive action, Carlzon introduced more dramatic change than many in his position would have dared. But it was precisely his bold leadership that positioned SAS today as a major global factor in the travel industry.

Carlzon clearly understood the complex of forces for change that his company faced, and his actions reflected a corporate philosophy well suited to winning the competitive battle in a service industry. He has a masterful understanding of the service industry and what it takes to succeed in it. By turning the traditional corporate pyramid upside down, Carlzon placed customers, not corporate executives, on top, followed by employees, then management. It doesn't take a Ph.D. to understand the ramifications of this game plan, but strangely enough, few other companies have tried it. With Carlzon's visible success, however, I suspect he will have many followers in the 1990s.

A 15-second encounter between a passenger and an employee is long enough to firmly plant an impression of the company in the passenger's mind. Carlzon, who knew where his kind of thinking about service delivery would lead, refers to these encounters as "moments of truth." When he began empowering his employees to make appropriate decisions during these moments of truth, things began to happen. Passengers walked away with smiles when they didn't have to wait for a supervisory sign-off on a decision. Employees began to take pride in their ownership roles as members of the SAS team. And lo and behold, profits began to appear on the bottom line.

When I joined Citicorp in 1985 as CEO of the Diners Club organization, my challenges and opportunities looked more like those of Jan Carlzon than Jack Welch's. Citicorp bought Diners Club in 1981 and was prepared to invest in a strategy to renew the business as a competitor to American Express in the travel and entertainment (T&E) market. I joined the business to take on the challenge of turning those aspirations into reality. For me, the excitement of the challenge lay in Citicorp's encouragement of bold thinking to accomplish this task. It was a golden opportunity to clear the decks and implement my vision of a leading-edge corporate culture.

Many of the philosophies we implemented are similar to those of Welch and Carlzon. The goal continues to be the creation of a customer-driven culture. My belief is that the customer must be the single dominant voice driving our actions. We divided the business into three profit centers structured around our three customer bases—individual cardholders, corporate card issuers, and establishment card acceptors—ensuring that resources were consolidated around serving each customer's needs. As part of our customer-oriented doctrine, we carefully empowered employees throughout the business. Those closest to our customers are empowered to do the right things, and everyone above the front line works to solidify our customer relationships.

Like Welch, I wanted to flatten our organization, ideally leaving no more than four layers of management. Aside from the obvious benefit of efficiency gains, I had even more fundamental aims. We were trying to overhaul the communication processes. By broadening each manager's span of control, I hoped to reduce the bureaucratic paper shuffling that typically plagues a business with too many layers and controls. Communication channels established across managerial lines would send the executional focus downward instead of upward through three or four management layers before a decision is made. Almost like trying to reverse a river's current, reversing the natural upward communication flow can be exhausting. But you can't have a customer-responsive organization if people are focused upward.

A declaration of this philosophy can get you a pat on the back; implementing it can get you stabbed in the back. Supporters somehow evaporate into thin air, and the loneliness of living with this decision is relieved only by the knowledge that it's right for the business and your customers. At Diners Club, I ensured that the changes we made were consistent and compatible. Flattening the organization reinforced the effects of empowering employees; both changes put decision-making at lower levels. As a result, we constantly wrestled with career path development for middle managers, whose jobs were eliminated or threatened by the reduction in corporate layers. Dealing with the personal and professional lives of others requires skill, understanding, and compassion.

Be prepared to confront challenges similar to those at Diners Club, no matter what level you're at in your company. I don't expect Diners Club to be a model for every issue you'll face any more than SAS or GE are perfect exemplars. Still, take advantage of the lessons these companies offer in overcoming the traumas of managing in a new corporate culture.

Implications for Middle Managers

Today there are more than enough examples of bold corporate redesign to enable middle managers to get a clear picture of what's to come. Organizations will continue to get *flatter,* with more diverse reporting relationships for those with people management responsibilities. Few will argue that a more *empowered* culture allows for efficient decision-making at the lowest possible level. The focus on *customer needs* will certainly intensify. *Leaders* of individual business units will take on new roles and responsibilities, reflecting their broader responsibility for the total business as *entrepreneurs.* Customers, suppliers, joint-venture partners, and competitors will all be *globally* defined, placing a premium on knowledge of what's going on beyond domestic markets. We can expect increasing *innovation in compensation structures* that promote a sense of ownership among all an organization's employees. And with ownership comes the renewed importance of taking *risks* in arriving at decisions and embracing the business as if it were your personal property.

The blinders are coming off, and the emerging picture is clearer than ever. For you, the big question is how your current company, or one you might join in the future, will adapt to these changes. Since change is driven by the unique circumstances, style, and temperament of leadership, you will have to translate these trends into predictions for your own environment.

How fast the management culture changes in your company will have a big effect on your career development program. But it should not dictate the fundamentals of that program. You must define the foundation skills that you're going to acquire, then use the pace of cultural change in your company to modify the tactics you use to acquire those skills.

Your first priority is to define the critical management skills you must have. In the next four chapters, I'll give you a list of skills that I think are imperative for the emerging culture. I'll also outline specific rules for building those skills and give you advice on how to get support from your company.

It's time to get specific on how to gain the upper hand on your career, so let's begin with the key management issue for success-ful career advancement—managing people relationships.

3

The First Key Experience: Strengthening People Relationship Skills

In January 1986 I made an organizational decision at Diners Club that dramatically affected career paths for our middle managers. If you haven't already experienced some of what I'm going to describe, you will, because it will occur frequently in the 1990s.

Financial disaster hovered over the business during my first year at the company's helm in 1985. We'd lost a great deal of money and had fallen substantially short of earnings delivery commitments. The powers-that-be in New York understood the complex causes of Diners Club's poor performance and didn't pressure me for a quick cure. Although infrastructure costs were out of line with our revenues, I avoided the temptation to make an across-the-board cut to get things back in order. But I did institute a total reorganization of the business to solve the infrastructure issue and simultaneously strengthen our decision-making capability.

Our solution permanently changed the company's culture. A radical flattening of the organization, dubbed "Four by Four," required all people managers to have at least four direct reports under them with no more than four layers of management in any area of the business. Bang—the first shot smacked hard but not where you'd expect. Although we did make some reductions in staff, the larger impact was felt by the 40 percent of our managers who traded people management responsibilities for direct front-line delivery of results.

All the planning on paper didn't prepare me for the ensuing emotional turmoil. Sure, these managers were thankful they still had jobs. But they viewed their new roles as a demotion, despite equivalent job grades and salaries. Every aspect of the previous culture married people management with career advancement, a marriage the Four by Four concept quickly annulled.

We sold the concept hard and preached that power is measured by what you do, not by the number of people reporting to you. We asked our employees to trust in our judgment that eliminating their people management responsibilities wouldn't derail their careers. Did many of our middle managers believe us? No. Hardly any other companies were visibly adopting such a radical position, so our managers felt exposed, shaken. They did, however, accept what we said.

That same request today would probably be much more positively received by the middle management work force. They're seeing and reading about the corporate restructuring principles that Peter Drucker and others promote. Drucker, in a January 1988 article in the *Harvard Business Review,* envisions the new breed of manager as a professional with information-processing skills and an ability to operate autonomously in an organization driven by specialization. In fact, he sees the organization operating much like a symphony orchestra: one conductor manages many players, each of whom is responsible for a specific function. Managers, or conductors, would be capable of coordinating the special talents of a vast number of information specialists, even though they wouldn't have the expertise to play the role of any of them.

The momentum toward flatter organizations has picked up speed since we made the move at Diners Club. In fact, the advice of management experts like Drucker has led many companies to go even further than Diners Club did in flattening their organizational structures. Despite the onset of a new culture, many of my middle managers still aren't convinced that the change was right for them. The lack of people management responsibilities created by delayering our organization remains the single largest human resource concern at Diners Club today. The problem is obvious from our annual attitude survey of all employees. It shows that morale is lowest among middle managers and that the overriding cause is their concern about career path options being limited by their lack of people management responsibilities. As you'll see, however, there's a new skill to be learned, people *integration,* that will be as important—even more so—than the traditional people management skills.

Changing Values for Managers

Traditional values die hard. After five years of cultural change, our Diners Club middle managers still cling to their cultural heritage. I suspect you do the same. But you need to dump the old values and do your people management thinking in the light of new ones. Better to see the light while the sun is rising than to scramble in the midday heat.

Forget the notion that people management skills are needed only by those with some sort of formal people responsibility. This was never the case, but the negative consequences of ignoring the issue if you don't manage direct reports will multiply as we face cultural shifts. To become properly oriented, think about the two basic roles traditionally associated with people management. The first is the classic managerial responsibility for direct reports, including such tasks as providing direction, creating job expectations, evaluating the performance of subordinates, and planning career paths. The second role is managerial responsibility for people integration; it focuses on the broader issue of how each person's work fits into the goals of the overall organizational unit.

Up until now, we've tended to make these two management functions into one role taken on strictly by individuals who have people to manage. In the future, the two roles will be separated. More managers will be judged on the second function—their people integration skills—and the classic direct-report management skills will be handled full-time by fewer people.

To be successful in the emerging culture, every one of you will be expected to strengthen your people integration skills because using those skills will increasingly determine how and where business gets done and how careers are made. As an example, imagine yourself in a specialized information function with no direct reports. Your boss might be responsible for 10–30 people, all with unique and independent roles to play. She's never going to know all the details of what each of you does, much less coordinate the day-to-day interfaces between you. Throw in the inevitable bottlenecks created by people in other departments who report to different bosses and you begin to see the real challenge to your people integration skills. You are the only one with the time and knowledge to do the job.

The idea behind flatter organizations is that people have the skills to work out solutions to their own problems by themselves. Taking the problems up the ladder won't fix them. You need people integration skills to work across the organization, sort out the issues among your peers, and get the right solution accepted by everyone affected. If this doesn't require people integration skills, I'm missing something.

Corporations that bet on the benefits of flatter organizations are effectively betting on the talents of their staff to integrate people across the organization, rather than up the hierarchy. The staff member without this ability will stick out. Ironically, the traditional hierarchy covered up people who were deficient in these skills because the boss could shield them by taking on total responsibility for people integration. But employees are being told less often what to do by a traditional boss and are increasingly expected to use their judgment in working across divisions and working with their peers to get things done.

Don't misread the impact of flatter organizations on people management skills. There will be fewer positions with formal responsibility for direct reports, and managers in those positions will have different assignments from those of the people manager in the traditional organization. Across the entire organization, however, there's no question that the essential role of people integration skills will be even more valued than it is today.

Based on the emotional reaction of the middle managers at Diners Club who lost formal people management functions, I know the arguments I'm making are hard to accept. Trust me, or the hundreds of others who flattened organizations and lived to tell about it. You can't go wrong building people integration skills as part of your professional strengths.

The strategy you adopt in accepting formal management responsibilities for direct reports should be very carefully thought out. Remember, people management assignments in the flatter organization structure will become a full-time responsibility that you earn because of your skills, not because you accumulate enough "at-a-boys." Superior people skills will be required from your first day on the job.

If you feel cozy where you are because your company isn't adopting any new principles, take off the blinders. Working in an environment where people management is granted as a perk is all well and good, but what happens if the company moves to a flattened structure? You could become a casualty. Either get busy building your people management skills to a level of absolute superiority or develop a long-range strategy to move into a role where management of direct reports isn't required.

The Empowerment Factor

Organizations have been eliminating layers of management long enough to be able to document the impact on people relationship issues. But another cultural change could become even more pervasive. In its purest sense, empowerment pushes authority and control down from the top of the traditional organization to the bottom. By adopting the principle of empowerment, managerial responsibility for direct reports becomes less a matter of control than of facilitation.

It's hard to inspire enthusiasm for the positive long-term benefits of a strategy that has such dire short-term implications for middle managers in particular. It takes time to establish support across the organization for moving forward on empowering efforts. Senior managers will face a major challenge as their companies try to combine the benefits of empowerment and a flattened structure. Middle managers who see the transition issues clearly can not only facilitate company and career goals but distinguish themselves in the process.

Much of middle managers' concern over flatter organizational structures and employee empowerment stems from the value placed on jobs and titles. People have historically judged a manager's job importance by the number of layers and people underneath him or her. Frontline jobs with no people responsibilities have been considered completely insignificant. We changed that perception at Diners Club by radically altering employee roles and the status given to job assignments through our efforts to empower all employees to be more responsive to customers. Part of the motivation to redefine job status emerged from a study we conducted of the jobs in which customer "touches" actually occur. Naturally, we believed these jobs to be the most important and wanted to recognize them as such. Who would have thought we'd discover that the mailroom was the most frequent point of customer contact? Further studies uncovered the fact that no one had ever been promoted *into* the mailroom. Such job positioning hardly seemed consistent with the goal of making empowerment real at Diners Club. We began to rectify the imbalance.

About this time, I was involved in a special project with Harvard Business School. Harvard wrote a case study on the Diners Club organization to be used in class discussions. I spoke to one of the classes about our strategy for executing the empowerment concept. When I described our findings about the mailroom, I threw out a challenge: following graduation, would anyone take a job at Diners Club to head the mailroom? I might as well have asked for volunteers to supervise garbage collection.

Frankly, I wasn't too surprised by this reaction; it was pretty symptomatic of traditional thinking about job value and status. Frontline jobs with no direct people management responsibilities have historically been given little status, regardless of how critical these jobs are to customer satisfaction. But the good news is that value structures are changing, and as they do, jobs high in customer contact will be rewarded with increased compensation, status, and security. But during the transition from the traditional to the emerging culture, talented people must be persuaded to move into these functions, and the people who already occupy them must begin to understand the increasing importance of their roles. Your goals should be to keep your eyes peeled for important frontline assignments as they open up and to strengthen the frontline teams that carry out these activities.

The barriers to embracing empowerment are enormous. At Diners Club, we have battle scars to show for our efforts, and our experience mirrors that of practically every company working toward this goal. Without question, the stress lands heaviest on middle managers who are asked to walk the fine line between getting the cooperation of frontline personnel and assuring top management that the business is under control. Those who successfully make the cultural transition invariably have superb people management skills. They must be good listeners and communicators both upward and downward in the organization. Other skills required of them include:

- understanding the limits of authority and action their bosses empowered them to take;
- communicating with and motivating subordinates to act in an empowered fashion within those limits;
- counseling subordinates and shaping the direction of their initiatives without controlling their activities; and
- making progress reports sufficiently detailed to retain support from above.

To accomplish all this regularly and successfully, you need well-developed people management skills. It's no wonder that many middle managers operating in traditional environments feel unrelenting stress.

You might think that empowerment removes the need for frontline people to play politics in the never-ending battle to reach timely decisions. Those with frontline knowledge of a situation most certainly must never miss a chance to take appropriate action, but empowerment also involves knowing when to ask for help. Employees acting as an island unto themselves will sink to the depths of Atlantis. The successful empowered employee will work hard to come to agreement with others about how to identify the times when help is needed and determine where to get it.

Communication demands will intensify because all employees will exchange information more frequently and informally than in the past. They will need to discuss important issues one on one, without waiting for the rumor mill to kick into high gear. Honest communication will become especially important as we see flatter, more empowered organizations. The heavily layered organization in which communication between management and employee is filtered and communication incompetence is hidden will disappear as greater emphasis is placed on powerful communication skills.

Six Rules to Develop People Management Skills

To help shape your people management skills, I'll give you a list of six rules. To make it easier to understand how to apply these rules, I'll also offer examples of how they have been played out in real business situations. Before you start studying the six rules, however, I'd like you to complete a quick audit of your company's orientation with respect to people management. You need to know whether your company culture is better characterized by traditional 1980s traits or by those of the emerging 1990s culture. Just review each of the 10 cultural characteristics in the list below and give your company one point for each accurate description of it from the "emerging" category.

Audit Your Company for People Management

Your Company	Traditional Culture	Emerging Culture
_____*	1. Performance ratings are based mostly on the tangible contributions individuals make personally.	Performance ratings are based mostly on the overall accomplishments of organizational units and task force teams in which individuals participate.
_____	2. Mentoring roles are not explicitly encouraged or rewarded.	People are expected to mentor and generally assist other employees in their career integration.
_____	3. Few people make lateral transfers across organizational lines or functional areas in the business.	Lateral transfers are a way of life.

*Score 0 point for Traditional Culture; 1 point for Emerging Culture.

Traditional Culture	Emerging Culture	Your Company
4. Fast-track managers hit the deck running on a new assignment, direct visible changes, and are ready for a quick promotion.	Fast-track managers take tough assignments over an extended time period and leave only after a permanent management team is in place to carry on the successful work.	———
5. Each department has its own physical and psychological territory within the company.	An outsider would have difficulty relating organizational reporting relationships to day-to-day behavior because people constantly interact across organization lines.	———
6. The company has no formal procedure to help people meet and network with peers from other parts of the organization.	The company brings managers together from different areas and expects them to build networks.	———
7. MBO or other goal-setting processes are created and approved between a boss and a subordinate with the focus on a narrowly defined job and specific transaction responsibilities.	MBOs often reflect goals shared with managers in other organizational units.	———
8. Most communication down the organization is written, and formal upward communications are very limited.	A large part of business communication is conducted face to face, and senior managers routinely hold discussions with employees many levels down from their direct reports.	———
9. Information meetings are discouraged because people have less time to get their work done as a result.	Managers are required to hold regular meetings with their direct reports to mutually exchange information on what's happening and why.	———
10. There is a high proportion of shredders to copiers in the company—much information is considered confidential and has restricted distribution.	There is an open attitude about sharing information if it helps someone do a better job.	———
		TOTAL

If the score for your company is 8–10, you should aggressively follow the rules for developing people management skills to accelerate your career development. Pay particular attention to the rules of people integration because these will be useful throughout your career.

If your company's score is 4–7, you should take reasonable risks in following the rules I've outlined. You don't want to become vulnerable when your newly developed skills are discounted by your boss. However, if the score is 0–3, be very careful. You still need to play by today's rules in a traditional culture that values delivering results more than people relationship skills.

The following rules cover relationship management and people integration skills in the broadest sense. As such, they are relevant to every middle manager, regardless of the specific role each of you might play in the emerging organizational culture.

Rule 1: Treat Every Idea from Another Employee as a Valuable Contribution and Make It Your Challenge to Bring It to Life

Many of the philosophical underpinnings of the emerging management culture are tied to one simple objective: unleash greater contributions from every single employee. The elimination of hierarchies, the drive to empower more employees, and the reduction of functional barriers between organization units are all designed to accomplish this objective. Whatever your position in your company's structure, your ability to facilitate those contributions from fellow employees will benefit you as much as them.

One manager from an entrepreneurial company told me: "I figured out a long time ago that if I wanted support for a project, I couldn't take a functional perspective. I mustn't shoot down any idea, even if I think I'm dead right—then we end up with nothing except volleys firing back and forth. I've seen time and again that greater awareness for the overall business comes from weighing each idea's potential contribution to the organization."

Mechanisms for employees to suggest new ideas for their company have certainly existed for a long time. But the traditional culture hasn't activated the creative juices to the same degree we're likely to see in the future. The mechanism in the traditional culture reminds me of the suggestion box I recently saw tacked to a tree on a golf course—the catch was that the tree was on a tiny island completely surrounded by water.

There are many factors that have blocked corporations from tapping the total contributions their employees might make. One of those blockages is the Machiavellian management philosophies that are ingrained in the traditional culture. In fact, many successful managers have built their careers by identifying and exploiting natural points of conflict between organizational functions. Arguing that the best solution to a business problem comes from testing competing theories, these individuals watch carefully as the functional adversaries verbally fight each other over the directions the business should take. These fights may be between marketing and production departments over the merits of a unique new product that requires tremendous special handling to produce. Or fights occur in functional areas, such as over the issue of whether marketing dollars should be allocated to advertising or trade promotion.

The Machiavellian conflict ends with winners and losers. It hurts to be on the losing side. Winning sometimes isn't much better because the effort expended to gain the victory sometimes leaves the winners too tired to relish their victory. In the era we're now entering, however, few organizations can afford either the luxury or the wreckage this management style creates. Indeed, the wreckage of this traditional decision-making process may be far more damaging to a company than the flattened morale of those who lose particular battles.

Adversarial processes teach people to hitch their managerial wagon to the functional units that have the strength to win most of the battles. Managers tend to line up behind safe, traditional, middle-of-the-road ideas and functions. How can you blame them? Who wouldn't prefer to have a small role in the winning business direction over sinking with a proposal that might make a lot of sense but stands little chance of prevailing?

The nonproductiveness of this situation is becoming increasingly apparent to senior executives, and they're worried about it. Besides not tapping the full creative resources of their employees, companies simply aren't achieving the rate of innovation they desire. Compared to the systems of many foreign competitors, particularly the Japanese, the existing U.S. system is obviously inadequate. Nothing drives change like adversity.

The Japanese success story has probably served as the single greatest catalyst for corporate rethinking of people integration issues. Although the different work ethic and cultural habits of the Japanese make their consensus management process difficult to adopt totally in corporate America, the fundamental principles can be applied here. Quality-circle techniques have been lifted from Japan by many U.S. companies with outstanding results. Ford Motor Company demonstrated the benefits of broad-scale employee participation when it threw out most of the standard design practices while creating the Taurus. Employee suggestions, from big ideas to subtle details, were incorporated into the design up front where they counted. The car has been the flagship of Ford's assault in the 1980s on General Motors' dominant position in the auto industry.

Ford's success was a cultural revolution for Detroit that wouldn't have occurred without open leadership at the top. As the emerging management culture takes hold, senior executives will place increasing importance on making sure their corporate environments foster creativity. The suggestion box will be moved to as convenient a location as possible, and the challenge to managers will be to stimulate the creativity of other employees.

This challenge is not limited to those employees you supervise. In the flatter organization, if you have customer contact or work as an information specialist, you will find yourself increasingly in contact with many different employees across the business. Every one of those contacts will be an opportunity for you to make something positive happen with the ideas generated by fellow employees.

Most important is the attitude you take toward an idea when it first arises. If you are from the Machiavellian school, your first instinct is to discount the idea, shoot it down, or treat it as nothing more than a corollary of something you had already thought of yourself. That kind of thinking is ingrained in many traditional management processes. You need to break out of it. Instead, listen with an open mind to what your colleagues have to say. Don't make negative judgments at all, if possible. At the very least, don't make them until you have explored every positive aspect of the idea. You'll be amazed at what can happen in your management meetings when you take this kind of leadership role in integrating people's ideas.

A manager from a major utilities company told me about a highly successful program one of her employees implemented. "When people were just beginning to look for employment security, rather than job security, one of our human resources team suggested having outside consultants advise on career development. She knew it would be a tremendous risk to go outside for assistance, but we simply didn't have the expertise in-house. I admitted the idea was intriguing but a bit scary; still, I let her run with it. So, through a consulting firm, she found successful managers at various levels who had positioned themselves well and hadn't just stayed in the same job forever. These managers she used to deliver the employee seminars.

"My gut reaction paid off. The seminars were constantly oversubscribed, and since they cost only half of what our internal training organization charged, we actually turned ourselves into a profit center, a first for any organization within our area. While everyone else was cutting budgets, I was able to put money back into the organization as a result of this program."

One of our Diners Club middle managers with a natural talent for supporting and building on the ideas of other managers showed me how far the process can go. I had been holding a series of informal breakfast meetings with middle managers, each with a topic defined by the managers who were attending. In this particular meeting, the topic was marketing. After some discussion, the group concluded that many Diners Club employees wanted to help market our products, but the mechanism wasn't in place to give them a chance. For example, employees sometimes patronized restaurants that didn't accept the Diners Club card. They wanted to try to sell the card to the restaurant but didn't know how.

One of the attendees asked if she could initiate a task force to more fully explore the idea. I supported the request immediately. She initiated brainstorming discussions with employees from all levels of the company. Many ideas came from these sessions, largely because this manager set the tone and created an environ-ment in which people knew their ideas counted. Out of the process we developed a permanent program called Club Ambas-sador. It's a system that gives our employees the tools to be a business "ambassador" anytime an opportunity arises to sell our products or services. The program recognizes and rewards every employee who participates in it. It's been a terrific addition to the business, thanks to one employee who built on a series of ideas and made sure they didn't get lost.

One reason it is difficult to maintain a creative environment is the natural conflict between the values of different functional units in a business. It is virtually impossible to organize a business that avoids functional conflicts completely. Directly or indirectly, you will inevitably witness ideas generated from one functional perspective being instantaneously rejected by those from another function. For example, legal department reviews of advertising copy almost always generate fights between the staff lawyer and the marketing manager over copy claims. To resolve this type of conflict, it is tempting to hand it over to a higher level manager who will give both combatants their marching orders. Unfortu-nately, that traditional solution often produces only winners and losers. But win-lose situations can be avoided if managers become far more sensitive to the people management issues.

I was fortunate to work with a man who is a master at integrat-ing functional strength while maintaining the integrity of each functional discipline. Gordon McGovern, CEO of Campbell Soup during most of my tenure with the company, time and again demonstrated his knack for accomplishing his business objectives in a nonconfrontational manner. Gordon created the business unit concept early in his tenure as CEO to segment the large, divisional organization into smaller, market-driven units. Each unit was headed by a general manager who had a clear mission to aggressively increase market position. To accomplish this, the general manager had full profit responsibility and control of all product development and marketing funds. Producing and deliv-ering business unit products, however, was the responsibility of a centralized manufacturing division that had a separate organi-zational reporting stream.

When this structure was established, I was given the business unit responsibility for beverages. This area was viewed as an enormous long-range opportunity for Campbell—yet the starting base was small and rather narrow, consisting of V-8 juice and Campbell tomato juice. As our Beverage Business Unit began working on aggressively expanding our business base, one idea struck us as a "quick hit" opportunity. Our existing products competed in the juice market, led by the sale of orange juice, most of which is sold either in frozen concentrate or refrigerated packaging forms. Our products, however, were almost exclusively sold in large cans on the dry grocery shelf. Why couldn't we expand our existing base by providing the product in the form consumers viewed as standard for juice packaging? We were off and running. That is, until we plowed into the manufacturing "mavens."

In fairness to manufacturing, the simple marketing idea of modifying packaging created a manufacturing nightmare. The technology, equipment, production methods, and distribution logistics were totally different for frozen concentrate and refrigerated forms of beverages. A complete manufacturing redesign was required to make the idea come to life. The size of the capital investment needed the support of manufacturing, which had a lot of clout in the organization on such decisions. Why? Simply put, manufacturing consistently put out a high-quality product at a lower cost than any competitor did, giving it a major say in key decisions driving the company's future.

Gordon McGovern knew all this, and also that a clash between the Beverage Business Unit and manufacturing was inevitable. He knew that in the end he'd play a major role in the resolution of the conflict. Manufacturing knew this as well. So it took a brilliant preemptive action that put us on the defensive. The senior manufacturing executive raised an important issue: since we were dealing with a specific brand product, namely V-8 juice, shouldn't the taste of the product be the same in all packaging forms? This was a perfectly appropriate concern from a manufacturing perspective, since maintaining quality consistency standards was this group's single most important objective. Maintaining a consistent taste for V-8 juice made sense to us, and so we supported this requirement as part of the planning strategy.

It wasn't long before the impact of this decision sent us reeling.

Completely transferring the V-8 flavor from a canned product into other forms turned out to be virtually impossible. We were in a corner. My instincts sent me to Gordon for counsel. His answer was quick and perfect. We knew most consumers squeezed lemon into V-8. He suggested we introduce the new forms with a taste of lemon juice, creating a different flavor expectation. We could get our package form testing under way without forcing the conflict with manufacturing into a win-lose situation.

I took Gordon's advice, and we eventually put our new product on the market. The frozen concentrate didn't prove a winner, but we successfully introduced the refrigerated form. Over time we even learned to get the flavor close enough to that of canned V-8 juice that the "touch of lemon" was no longer needed.

Gordon McGovern's ability to spot peaceful solutions to functional conflicts was almost second-nature. His personal style facilitated the process, but his skill at integrating functions came from many years of work in the various management positions he'd occupied. This is a valuable management asset because it's extremely rare.

The demand is on for people who can facilitate cooperation and the integration of ideas among units. Roll up your sleeves and start practicing these skills in your day-to-day interaction with coworkers. It will take time for you to develop your skill at drawing out and supporting good ideas, but it will be worth the effort. You can begin immediately by switching on a red light in your mind whenever you witness or actively participate in the destruction of a colleague's idea because it happens to be in opposition to your group's thinking.

Rule 2: Share Information across Organizational Boundaries, and Build and Use Networks among Peer Managers

Following this rule on networking is one of the most significant ways in which people integration skills can benefit your career.

As noted earlier, Peter Drucker forecasts that information

management skills will be the key to future professional roles. As these roles take specific shape, Drucker believes we will see a major acceleration in the flattening of corporate organization structures.

Drucker's vision of jobs designed around independently managed data relating to a specific function is already happening. With the advanced development of management information systems (MIS), all employees have much greater access to the right information to do their jobs better, and the software and technology to drive this are likely to improve even faster in the future.

As difficult as it has been to create truly user-friendly MIS technology, it has already started to bring about organizational change in companies. In the future we can expect to see even faster changes in job definitions and in organizational reporting structures as companies work to capitalize on the opportunities before them. One thing is sure: middle managers will be squarely in the middle of the process.

One virtually certain consequence of changing structures is that corporations will abandon their focus on narrowly defined management functions as a way of organizing responsibilities. Instead of accepting the classic functions, such as production, marketing, and finance, corporations will be composed of many specialized functions driven by information integration or decision integration. This change will put great pressure on the new working relationships across functions. Corporations simply can't be competitive if they stick with the slow and inflexible process of rolling business decisions up the production, marketing, and finance channels, with a top management steering committee standing guard to resolve the occasional conflicts between the core functions.

I expect to see many new hybrid functions in the companies of the future. They won't necessarily be functions that come out of the latest books on organizational theory. Instead, they will be driven by the specific needs of a particular business operating in a unique environment. The functions will come and go as needed to do things right at a particular point in time.

Hybrid functions have already been created at Diners Club since we've flattened the organizational structure, built better

MIS to support frontline decisions, and deemphasized some of the traditional functional focuses. One special function we created handles a special kind of customer relationship problem. When we were seeing delinquent payments by some of our cardholders, we weren't sure if we should treat them as a collections or a customer service issue. The solution was to create the Integration Functional Unit, which is made up of staff trained in both areas. Besides enabling each function to address customer needs individually, we solved an interface problem between the two without challenging the role of either one.

As a middle manager, you have an opportunity to prepare yourself for the transition to the emerging organizational structure, or to even aggressively facilitate the changes. Whether you play it safe or aggressively is your call. But either way, you must begin the process of building managerial networks across your organization. If you start the process now and are aggressive in building solid and often nontraditional peer relationships—for instance, between employees in finance and those in R&D—you have the chance to define some of the emerging new functions that will be best suited to your company.

At Diners Club, the Integration Functional Unit was originally proposed by a team of middle managers. Perhaps through carefully sharing information with other middle managers on what each of you do, how you do it, and how it potentially relates to your areas of responsibility, you can define new functions that will also get the attention and support of senior management. Someone is going to start to define these functions, and it's likely to be the individual who first crosses the organizational boundaries and discovers the opportunities. Why not lead the charge?

Being a middle management leader and networking across organizational boundaries can also put you in a position to develop business-oriented goals for yourself that have a much bigger impact on the overall organization. If you have been a pioneer in forming networks in your company at your management level, the odds are that your boss isn't even aware of the linkages you have discovered. If you use your network relationships well, you and your peer managers in other units can redefine your operating goals and also change the whole goal-setting process.

Many traditional companies operate a goal-setting or MBO

process that is driven strictly by hierarchical reporting relationships. In other words, the annual goals for an employee are negotiated strictly between that person and his or her superior. That process will not last in the emerging culture, and you may have an opportunity to visibly lead in the campaign to quicken its demise.

We restructured our MBO process at Diners Club from top to bottom largely because our middle managers found the traditional process was stifling them and preventing them from doing the right things for the business. Diners Club had a strong MBO-oriented culture when I joined the company; all the classic conditions for functional wars were firmly in place. There was a strong link between MBOs and performance evaluations, but the process itself seemed to destroy chances to implement programs that required support from other organizational units.

Our breakthrough came when we changed the entire MBO negotiation system. MBOs had been negotiated strictly up and down functional organizations. Each manager wrote his MBOs to quantify key functional requirements from the operating plan. Based on the plan and the MBOs, the process was then pushed down to lower levels. A link up and down the organization on MBOs was maintained, but issues that required shared objectives across different functional units were never resolved. Consequently, some of the company's most critical businesswide objectives never appeared in anyone's MBO because they didn't really fit into one specific functional area.

With the start of a new fiscal year, we decided to wipe the slate clean on the old MBO procedure. First we reviewed the strategic and operating plan to establish a common understanding of business objectives. Then we asked each manager to develop objectives shared with other managers that reflected their joint management responsibilities. When the process was developed enough to link MBOs across functions at the top of the organization, the managerial MBOs at lower levels were relatively easy to adapt. Thus, the conflicts over shared MBOs were dramatically reduced, and the MBO tie to business priorities was significantly increased.

The process was so successful that we took a second step to create greater integration among managers. We introduced a formal management process in which task forces were established to manage solutions to cross-functional business problems. The task force teams for each problem included not only individuals with the expertise to solve the problem but others who had hands-on learning experience from their participation on the team. A deeper managerial understanding of the issues facing the business emerged with the development of collective responsibility for problem resolution.

The final step of the process involved performance appraisals for the managers. We instituted a system in which the top 50 managers were evaluated as a group, signaling that performance would now be measured by a collective ability to contribute to the key business issues, not by individual ability.

Some of you might be in a position to facilitate changes in your MBO systems, your methods of managing task force projects, or your performance evaluation process. I encourage you to look for a chance to lead change in directions similar to those we took at Diners Club. Plan ahead so you can capitalize on the opportunity when it does arrive.

Rule 3: Empower People Whenever You Can But Always Be Clear about Your Business Reasons for Doing So

It is entirely possible that the word *empowerment* won't last through the transition to the emerging corporate culture, even though the concept is one of the primary drivers of change. *Empowerment* is becoming a common word in the management vocabulary but is seldom understood to mean the same thing by the various people who use it. That's a big danger. There are so many value-loaded connotations to empowerment that it may fall out of vogue if managers get too frustrated when they actually try to implement it.

When employees first get a general description of the empowerment concept, there is usually fairly universal enthusiasm for it. Almost everyone thinks about it in terms of the personal gains it makes possible. Almost no one thinks at first about the obligation to empower subordinates. When that aspect is introduced, the euphoria about newfound freedoms diminishes. "Am I really willing to fully empower those below me in the organization?" Many managers aren't so sure how they feel about that aspect of empowerment. It can be very difficult to convince them that their subordinates' empowerment doesn't lead to their own "depowerment."

Middle managers have an especially difficult time reconciling the various aspects of empowerment. They can easily see themselves as a conduit for empowering the front line of the organization, with ultimate control continuing to rest at the top. They believe they have been squeezed into a position of holding neither much power nor much control.

One middle manager told me about the bitter reaction of his peers when the concept was introduced in his company. "Everyone was extremely resistant. Conversations went along the lines of, 'You can't trust hourly employees; they're not interested in anything but getting their paychecks,' or, 'If we don't have the power to supervise, we'll end up with sloppy production.'" Another manager related that miscommunication about empowerment and a lack of appropriate training "merely increased the already intense conflict in our company. Now we often see our frontline people take the attitude, 'Okay, you've empowered me. So I'm empowered to ignore you if I so choose,' or, 'I'm empowered to look to only those things that relate to taking care of my piece of the business or other measurements that belong to my area.' They're afraid of being given too much to do." Managers in this company were also afraid that what they were really being measured against wasn't getting done.

There is no question that empowerment can shake the self-esteem of many managers. The truth of the matter is that empowerment does not grant an individual wide-open freedom to act as he or she pleases. "How can you stop me if you empowered me?" is a manager's typical response to the first questions about his or her use of empowerment. But empowered employees must be motivated to act in the best interest of the business or the concept simply spells anarchy. No one is very excited about anarchy as a solid management concept for the 1990s.

The single hardest part of properly empowering employees is

making them completely understand the effect of empowerment on their power to make decisions to take action. Once that understanding is acquired, managers usually ask a series of related questions about empowerment execution. Do employees really have the relevant information, tools, and training to act successfully relative to goals and objectives? If they don't, what will it take to make those resources available to them? Do we negate all the potential benefits of empowerment by trying to upgrade everyone to the skill and knowledge standards of the managers who had the decision responsibilities before empowerment occurred? These are very tough questions, but they must be answered if an organization is to proceed with empowerment implementation.

Today almost all companies with an empowered culture stress the ownership principle more than any other as the primary motivation that unleashes employee innovation. After looking at their own jobs and at what's going on around them, it isn't difficult to get employees to ask, "If I personally owned this entire organization, would I really do things the way they're being done today?" The question is relevant to employees at every level. The market research professional should consider whether he wants a 30-page survey of customer attitudes, at $50,000 a crack, or, if the money is truly his to spend, whether he'd rather spend it in some other area that could perhaps reap greater benefits. The manager who calls an unproductive, weekly, two-hour staff meeting of 20 relatively bored individuals could rethink the options. The salary costs alone of this meeting probably exceed $100,000 a year—a sum that undoubtedly would receive a lot more attention if the manager was spending his or her own money on the meeting.

Obviously, if an ownership principle works best in implementing an empowerment philosophy, employee-owned companies have a tremendous advantage. The empowerment philosophy isn't theoretical to these employees. Indeed, studies that have documented productivity improvements in organizations that have gone through a true employee buy-out have pinpointed empowerment behaviors as a major factor in those improvements. One cautionary note, however: the employee-owned company must adopt a philosophy that permits employees to act as responsible owners of the business. A number of organizations that created total or modified employee-ownership structures never changed their operating philosophy. If you are looking for a role model for how to benefit from empowerment, look carefully at those organizations whose operating concept mirrors the financial structure of employee ownership. Look at Avis. It underwent an ESOP conversion in 1987 and leveraged the new employee ownership attitude with new television advertising in which a satisfied customer points to an Avis representative, and says, "I know the owner." If you're able to get some firsthand experience with such a company, you'll probably find it to be very enlightening.

Communication is critical to the process of empowering employees. No business can reap the benefits of empowerment unless empowered employees act in a spirit of ownership about their new responsibilities and authorities. But you can't expect them to act like owners if they remain cut off from key information. The burden of maintaining communication rests with managers at every level. The efforts of those managers charged with formal people management responsibilities are the most important, but everyone must make a similar commitment to maintaining communication in the flatter, decentralized operating structure.

Although you can readily start to instill an ownership spirit in your own functional area by constantly asking, "If it were your own business, would you do that?" it's a lot easier if that spirit pervades your company. We decided to make that commitment at Diners Club, even though we clearly were a subsidiary of a much larger organization. Despite the financial technicalities of ownership, in a very real sense the Diners Club employees were the company's owners. No one doubted that the company's destiny was totally dependent on the employees. So why not build on that idea? We did it through an ongoing communication mechanism called "Take Stock in Diners Club."

Our communication process treated Diners Club employees, in effect, as stockholders in the business. Each quarter I presented a report to the employees on the company's status. We were candid, balancing news about our accomplishments and successes with news about our shortfalls. Although the long-term benefits would become clear, we couldn't have chosen a worse time to make our first presentation.

Just one week before, we'd made a business decision that left a number of our employees looking for new jobs. The rumor mill went into high gear, and anxiety levels increased daily. While we could honestly discuss the status of the business and the issues it faced, we couldn't give people comfort on the most urgent question in their minds—would they continue to have a job with Diners Club?

As it turned out, the bad timing demonstrated the real value of making sure that all empowerment activities remain focused on business. The first Take Stock in Diners Club presentation went off as scheduled. I gave a candid assessment of the entire business situation and made the commitment to do everything possible to find jobs in the company for those affected by our recent decision. In a question-and-answer session we demonstrated our willingness to address employee concerns publicly, which did more to move the program along than anything else.

What was most amazing about that first presentation was that it enabled our human resources staff to get to work trying to solve the individual career problems created by our business actions. Everyone worked together, confident that they had the authority to take specific action that could facilitate other people's careers. Because of the way the whole process was handled, from publicly explaining the rationale for our business actions to empowering our frontline human resources staff, a potential disaster was headed off and benefits were reaped instead. Many employees who might otherwise have accepted outside offers stayed with the business in other capacities. The turnaround of the business was due in no small part to our handling of this critical situation. That turned out to be my first real experience with the benefits of employee empowerment. It gave us the confidence to move even more aggressively into this style of management.

Diners Club may have been lucky with the tie-in of its communications about downsizing with its empowerment efforts. Many companies faced with similar traumatic reactions to downsizing decisions have not fared as well. A breakdown of the communication process has usually been to blame.

AT&T is a classic example of an organization that paid a stiff price for sloppy handling of communication. Following deregulation and restructuring, AT&T was ready to launch a massive layoff program in 1984. Top management, however, allowed the news to leak to the press before notifying employees. The problem intensified when the company released ad hoc information about who would stay and who would go. Employees panicked, and the company's growth strategy, scheduled for implementation after the downsizing actions, was disrupted. Today, morale at AT&T is still low.

The business press these days also gives prominent coverage to the lack of frank communication from executives to middle management. Articles feature candid conversations with managers frustrated by corporate handling of career issues. The seriousness of this was illustrated by comments from senior executives like General Motors chairman Roger Smith. In *Business Week* (Sept. 12, 1988), Smith referred to rank-and-file managers as the "frozen middle"—that is, they have been unwilling to commit to changes he's tried to bring to GM. In response to Smith's comment, a GM manager asked, "If we're frozen, who left us out in the cold?" A middle manager from Manufacturers Hanover Trust Company put his finger on one of the basic problems associated with communicating key information about business directions. His greatest frustration as a middle manager is his inability to answer basic questions from his staff. Torn between not wanting to give away information they shouldn't have and wanting to be able to tell them, "Hey, I don't know what's going on!" he can't give advice on staff career paths when he doesn't have any advice for himself.

If there is a large communications gap between senior managers and middle managers in an organization, empowering employees will be virtually impossible. Bide your time or change jobs if you face that situation and are eager to start using empowerment concepts as a people management approach.

But if you face this problem simply because your senior managers are unaware of their communication shortfalls, you should consider being the first to get the ball rolling. Sometimes pushing top management to clarify the organization's business philosophy and operating expectations is all that's needed to break the logjam. Assess the attitudinal climate before you take this initiative, but if the timing is right, it could be a big opportunity for you. If you take the issue on, be ready to quickly use an empowerment approach with your organization to prove the benefits of clearer direction and communication from the top.

As you establish business rationales for empowerment action within your organization, provide your subordinates with information relevant to them on where the overall business is headed strategically. I am not talking about giving them confidential information or asking them to plow through detailed plans and programs. But if you really want them to commit to the changes you envision, don't surprise them with announcements that completely rattle their comfort zone. Instead, make employees active participants in the changes taking place. Get them involved in projects with a direct impact on the changes being made and constantly keep them informed. The pace of change can be frightening if they don't have time to prepare for it. Giving them that time will create an army of active advocates instead of concerned reactionaries.

The value of keeping people informed about business strategy was demonstrated during the turnaround period at Diners Club. The business had been losing money for years, and its market share was rapidly eroding. It was critical that all employees be able to relate to our turnaround program to help eliminate as many doubts as possible. So I designed a progress chart to help reduce doubt about our chances for success. I spelled out the goals for three different phases:

1. *Control*—to achieve basic financial, operating, and product delivery each time we promise them
2. *Profitability*—to get the business in the black
3. *Revenue Growth*—to have a sufficiently strong position in the key market segments in which business growth was under our control

Our target was to achieve each phase's goals in two years. Once our turnaround phases were established, all major communication to our employees related to our turnaround progress. More important, as we moved from one phase to the next, our communication allowed employees to understand where the organization was headed so they could get ready to participate.

Because we communicated this general information throughout the organization, our middle managers were able to focus on areas where empowerment would be most productive as we moved through each phase of the turnaround. No one was confused by the role changes brought on by empowerment; indeed, we found that middle managers and their empowered employees were well ahead of the priorities being set by senior management. For example, during the profitability phase, managers worked with and empowered service representatives to creatively solve the issue of multiple contacts from our cardholders. Every time a cardholder needed more than one contact with us to resolve a service problem, customer satisfaction deteriorated and our costs increased. Often the multiple contact problems were caused by unusual service needs that required the involvement of more than one organizational area. The service reps and their managers designed procedures to eliminate most of the multiple contact problems. As a result of their creativity, service levels improved and costs were reduced.

When the business turned to the revenue growth phase of the turnaround, we immediately saw a change in the empowerment focus of our middle managers and service reps. Instead of concentrating on multiple service contacts, the new focus was on designing systems the service reps could use to supply information to our cardholders on products and services they might not know we offered. In effect, the service reps transformed themselves into sales agents for the business, tactfully building relationships with customers while they simultaneously solved particular service needs. Their cross-selling activity obviously added some costs to our servicing function, but it was completely consistent with our focus at that time on increasing revenue for the business.

Managing an empowerment concept successfully is extremely difficult. It takes knowledge about the business's overall directions, an ability to translate that knowledge into information relevant to the employees being empowered, and constant communication with employees to ensure they are comfortable with the level of responsibility their new roles offer. To make the whole thing work, managers must be constantly on their toes.

The benefits of empowerment are enormous, but they don't come free. Any manager who thinks empowerment passes directly from senior executives to the front line with no involvement from middle managers has not worked in a truly empowered culture. Managers who are serious about making the concept work within their organization have plenty to do. You'll get the balance of managerial involvement right only by practicing the empowerment philosophy. Grab your opportunities, and start practicing.

Rule 4: Communicate in All Directions—Inform Upward, Empower Downward, and Network Outward

One of the essential differences between the emerging culture and the traditional one will be our reliance on people rather than systems and procedures to drive company success. The flatter organizational structures, the empowerment of the work force, and the customer-driven focus will all combine to reduce our preoccupation with formal procedures and rules for getting things done. In the emerging culture, we will strive relentlessly for meaningful communication among all employees. Operating rules will be more informal and will arise out of the communication networks instead of being imposed upon them.

The cultural shift will create great communication challenges for every manager. Success as both a people manager and a people influencer absolutely depends on your ability to effectively use communication processes in all directions within your organization. Recognize that fact up front, and start working aggressively on your communication skills. Communication is a two-way street; your listening skills need to be developed as much as your speaking and writing capabilities.

As communication processes become much more efficient and effective, we can expect employees to gain broader insight into relevant activities across the organization. One of the greatest corporate benefits of the improved understanding will be reduced conflict between functional areas. I can make this claim with a fair amount of confidence, having spent four years as a graduate student at the Wharton School studying why some conflicts intensify and others subside. My work was sponsored by the U.S. Arms Control and Disarmament Agency, an organization with obvious interest in such issues.

The meticulously organized literature on conflicts, which incorporates a broad range of scientific approaches to the issue, can be boiled down to a fairly simple generalization. You've heard it before, although perhaps not in this context. The Golden Rule, "Do unto others as you would have them do unto you," tells us how we ought to behave. The actual behavior of people in conflict situations, however, is better summarized as, "Do unto others as you believe they would have done unto you." A slightly different twist.

We too often assume that our motives are understood as pure. From our own point of view, we are acting responsibly and in the best interest of our company. Unfortunately, data from research suggest that we interpret ambiguous actions from "the other side" as hostile and aggressive. We incorporate this interpretation into our own responses, as we believe the other side would do in our situation. And so, of course, they do. At this point the conflict is off and running. The typical conflict could be avoided by carefully clarifying the intentions of the parties involved. A manager who controls meetings—who, for instance, determines when meetings are necessary—plays a vital role. Meetings are extremely important to the process of neutralizing potential conflicts arising from misunderstood intentions. But it's useless to try to gain agreement out of any meeting if there is confusion about the motivations behind actions or statements.

As you use memos and meetings to clarify understandings and eliminate ambiguous expectations, you'll see your communication becoming more effective. If you are to acquire the skills necessary in the emerging culture, you must be able to clearly define and control communication expectations. You will need to develop your own set of Golden Rules that help you understand how people are acting and what it takes to turn them in a preferred direction.

Over the years, companies have had many different attitudes about the value of open communication and networking among employees. But basically there are only two positions: you believe either that employees should have wide-ranging relationships throughout the company and an understanding of what's going on overall, or that no one needs anything more than specific knowledge about whatever is critical to their job responsibilities.

I agree with the companies that take a broader view of the value of network communications, even when they aren't very efficiently executed. The more liberal companies believe that the knowledge gained by their employees will pay dividends in the decision-making perspectives they maintain.

Delta Airlines is a good example of the liberal communications philosophy. It has practiced that philosophy in a number of ways for many years, but one representative incident has always stuck in my mind. At the height of the energy crisis in the mid-1970s, the federal government allowed all airlines to cut back on the number of flights they offered. The logic was simple: load factors would increase and fuel consumption would decrease. Every airline jumped at the idea, but Delta was the only major carrier that didn't lay off people in conjunction with the reduction. Although it recognized that excess staff would result, Delta also envisioned the opportunities the situation would unfold.

Delta explained the turn of events to its employees, identified the excess time that would be created, and asked all of them to use their portion of that time to learn more about other areas of the Delta system. Pilots spent time with baggage handlers to gain a better understanding of the inevitable plane delays caused when baggage wasn't loaded. Baggage handlers spent time with check-in personnel to witness similar impacts on their operations. It was a simple idea: the more people know about how others accomplish their objectives, the better able they are to work together to deliver the best customer service. Passengers noticed and appreciated the difference, as did employees—so much so that when the airline later suffered a financial setback, employees passed the hat and purchased a new plane as part of Delta's fleet refurbishing.

The benefits of advocating open communication will increase as the new culture unfolds. Flatter structures will force more horizontal communication among employees. In hierarchical businesses, informal communication can efficiently filter up and down because bosses have only a few people to keep informed. But in flatter structures with wider managerial span of control, the communication process must work very well, beginning with keeping the story straight and accurate. Don't rely on ad hoc, informal communications processes to do the job in a flat structure.

As a middle manager, you can play a real leadership role in facilitating communication across organizational lines that are out of your direct reporting channel. Become more sensitive to your formal and informal interactions in the organization. If you take communication seriously, you will have no use for ad hoc bull sessions that have no agenda or expected outcome.

Raise your expectations for every meeting you attend, particularly those you initiate, and every memo you write. Too many communication vehicles today are ineffective or time-consuming. For instance, a phone call can replace a memo and at the same time be more personal and to the point. Also, don't impose lengthy meetings on people who have no constructive role to play in them. The sooner the waste of time stops, the better. In the emerging culture, such waste will be replaced with more focused communication conducted at even higher levels of intensity than we experience today. The effectiveness of communication should be much greater because purposes will be more clearly established.

If you increase your ability to facilitate constructive communication, you'll have a real leg up when you enter meetings that have no organizational ties restricting the discussion. You will also be in a position to play a very meaningful role in facilitating communication upward in the organization. There is very little argument about the importance of senior management leadership in establishing a truly empowered employee culture. It is almost impossible for a major functional area of a company to isolate itself and empower its employees without corporate support. But middle managers will have great opportunities to accelerate the move to an empowered culture by being the ones to bring issues to the attention of those senior managers who can initiate philosophy changes in the business.

In the traditional culture, senior managers simply don't get good feedback on what it takes to generate creative energy in their organization. The flow of communication is largely downward, and senior executives are simply layered out of the forces and conditions that really drive employee energies. One of the classic traditional communication battles is still being fought at a large midwestern manufacturing company. Two of the company's managers spoke of the many times the company's communication policy, or lack thereof, thwarted product innovation.

"Within our corporation, there's a culture that says you don't tell management the truth," one of the managers divulged. "You tell them what they want to hear. For example, when we're dealing with the release of a product during a senior management meeting, the director giving the report will tell the executive committee that everything is on target—that everything's fat, dumb, and happy—regardless of what the situation really is.

"Meanwhile, senior management tells the world that the product is great, here it comes, it'll be on time, and it will do wonderful things for the customer. All of a sudden we come to the release date and we don't have anything. In many cases we don't release a product that was critical to the company, or we release one that wasn't ready. So the product fails, and management comes down hard and wants to know why we didn't inform them about the problems in advance so they could have taken appropriate action. Except they wouldn't take action other than screaming about who did what in an incompetent manner.

"And yet, if anyone is brazen enough to suggest that there are, indeed, problems, they're shot on the spot, and someone else is brought in who tells management exactly what they want to hear.

"The successful manager in our company gives the executive officers the illusion that what they *think* is going on, *is* going on. In the meantime, we try to meet the market's demands and hope senior management doesn't get in the way."

Needless to say, this company is not benefiting from being so mired in a traditional environment. You can be the catalyst to accelerate positive change in your company if you're in control of your communication processes and if you choose your timing well. Don't miss any upward communication opportunity.

Not that the benefits automatically or easily accrue to the companies committed to inaugurating the empowered employee culture. Diners Club senior managers took the lead in ushering in the new culture, but our methods of bringing the empowerment message to the employee population simply weren't working. The proliferation of communication vehicles and incentive programs was more confusing than rewarding to our employees. It took a group of middle managers to first identify the problem and then point out the right solution. The group happened to be working on a task force assignment to create a new umbrella advertising campaign for Diners Club. Although their work focused on what would make sense to our external customer markets, they also created the unifying solution to our internal employee empowerment programs.

The middle managers proposed that our advertising campaign work around the slogan, "We take care of business." The campaign's promise to our customers was simultaneously a call to action for our employees who had to deliver on the promise. The task force made the suggestion that we use actual employees in our ads to demonstrate that the "we" in the campaign slogan literally represented the people in our business.

The task force idea was immediately endorsed at the senior management level. Employee energy level improved noticeably as soon as word got out about the advertising campaign strategy. I'm sure we would have missed the idea had it not been generated by a group of middle managers who saw in detail what we needed to bring off the empowerment promise. By pushing communication upward in the organization, they provided the critical input that really got empowerment off and running at Diners Club. Don't miss out on your chance to act as a similar catalyst in your organization.

But your role in downward communication is as critical as communicating upward or across organizational boundaries. Any employee who formally reports to you will view you as the representative of senior management, even though you occupy a middle management position. If that employee's trust in the system breaks down, you must be the communication bridge that stands firm while trust is rebuilt. You must listen to his or her concerns and then resolve those concerns.

The greatest opportunities to bring communication benefits to your company will occur in situations that present the greatest risks. If you believe in more open communication, seek out the toughest issues to demonstrate its benefits. Gamble on as much open communication as possible, and provide it upward and downward simultaneously. Employees are powerfully motivated when they believe they are getting the straight scoop from the top. The more they understand about how they fit into the larger corporate environment, the more motivated they become to make positive contributions.

No matter how far you are from the CEO, you can still facilitate communication in peer and subordinate discussions. At these levels you have the choice of either enhancing or neutralizing open communication. A middle manager once told me about a cartoon hanging in his office. It pictured the boss sitting at his desk with a clenched first and a scowl on his face; the caption read, "My God, they did exactly what I told them to do." This same manager recounted his frustrations when trying to open the communication channels in his own company, explaining that the cartoon is all too real in his organization. Company information flows upward, and the boss dictates instructions downward. In cases such as these, directives often don't provide all the vital details for the actions the boss wants people to take, because he forgets he's the only person who has access to the whole picture. Too often, good people don't execute orders intelligently because they don't know what else is going on that specifically relates to their directives.

Through habit, or lack of knowledge, or the culture the senior manager is working in, middle managers can feel as if they're standing in silos where the only light comes from above and the only instructions come straight down. While stacks of information pile up, each separate piece is lost, missed by the people who need it. But the effective manager will openly communicate with other managers to allow information to reach all levels.

Make no mistake about how difficult it is for those in people management roles to alter cultural values. The challenges aren't over, but the foundations are now in place: empowerment is now an accepted management principle. Corporate leaders of the 1990s will earn their reputations by creating an environment that turns managers from focusing attention on how to impress those up above to empowering all employees to serve customers. They must literally reverse the job value structures and philosophy of advancement in their corporations. The returns will be large for those who make this shift before their competitors, but the challenges in doing so are great. How can you help ignite this change in your company if it gets the empowerment bug?

If you operate in a traditional corporate culture, you could become vulnerable when you aggressively try to improve communication in your company. Your investment of time and energy to establish and build on effective communication links across, upward, and downward in your organization will be considerable. I'm convinced that if you develop the skills to use these communication links purposefully, there will be true payoffs for your business. But it will be difficult to get unenlightened senior managers to attribute those payoffs to any single individual or process. Your new role may be responsible for conflicts never materializing or for cross-functional business projects going particularly well and too smoothly to attract attention.

Nevertheless, a senior manager may ask you one day, "I know you are very busy and involved in a great many things across the business, but what *exactly* have you done yourself to make a difference to the bottom line?" That question should never be asked about people management processes in the emerging culture, but it is often the first question in the traditional one. Questions just like that one drive people managers out of the organization. When the squeeze is on in a traditional culture, contributions to people management are often one of the last considerations in decisions about which resources "we simply must keep" and which "are expendable if we have to have cutbacks." Companies facing hard times today aren't about to get radical in their thinking. The lone specialist working by himself on something relevant to today's survival is apt to be rewarded over the manager who's working to build solid people relationships to achieve long-term goals.

A manager I know who supervises the financial unit of a large real estate developer has had to deal with a renewed interest in traditional values brought on by economic downturns affecting his company. He told me that of approximately 70 middle managers, 25 percent either lost their jobs in the past year or were forced to move into different assignments. His frustration was apparent. "All those people who are gone fell under the management profile of skilled people managers," he confided, "and with all the lip service given to people skills in the 1990s, they don't understand why their careers haven't been a success. I myself don't see any payback in developing people relationships. Perhaps a few years ago it would have been important, but new dynamics affecting corporate America are putting pressure on our senior managers. They're no longer willing to make extra investments to achieve long-term benefits. When the company tells us priorities are on short-term successes, we don't feel obliged to continue taking risks, and that includes devoting much time to the people side of the business."

This manager isn't alone. When your company is confronting such economic pressures, being a facilitator of effective communication is probably too intangible a quality upon which to secure your position. So be very careful about your timing and how much you invest in your communication capabilities. I give you that warning, recognizing the irony of the fact that communication is one of the most important drivers of success in the emerging culture. Timing is everything.

Rule 5: Build Your People Reputation on Trust and Cooperation

Yesterday's manager development process involved recruiting a class of new corporate managers every spring from undergraduate and MBA programs. The new recruits worked through parallel assignments in a company for 5–10 years, during which time they were ranked in comparison to their peer group. It was a competitive system that worked well in weeding out candidates, but it had a major flaw. Those who got ahead often did so at the expense of other managers. The old competitive attitude stipulates that for every winner there has to be a loser.

Today the fast-track middle manager moves into the executive ranks increasingly because of his or her skill at integrating and synthesizing the inputs of others, not at knocking them down. Unfortunately, many managers who set out on the fast track never acquire this skill. They are the sharks who still don't understand why the dolphins are getting ahead. And to the untrained eye, their behaviors are similar. A closer look, however, reveals distinct, unmistakable differences.

Even if you haven't experienced the shark breeding ground of management talent in your own organization, I'm sure that in other settings you've seen plenty of sharks who instinctively operate by traditional principles. The traditional culture encouraged more sharks than dolphins as managerial models. But today dolphins are preferred, and sharks who want to succeed will have to change their habits early in their careers. *Trust* and *integrity* are words you will hear often from now on, and if your reputation hints more of Jaws than Flipper, get to work. Don't wait until corporate sharks are an endangered species, when they won't be handed many new opportunities. A few sharks may still make it to the top, but would success really be worth the burden of having a ruthless reputation, when you might have, instead, accomplished your goals as a dolphin?

An acquaintance of mine recounted his struggle to undo internal competitive forces that were taking their toll on productivity in his organization. "The person who held the job before me was recognized for being extremely knowledgeable, but lacked the skills or foresight to get everyone working together. The prevailing attitude was, 'The more I can get you fighting with one another, the more you'll accomplish and the more successful our group will become.' Distrust and competition had reached an unhealthy level.

"I began to hold regular discussions with the staff, almost pleading with them to tell me what was going on—not just what they thought I wanted to hear. It took some getting used to on their part, especially for two managers who were at odds with one another. I took these two aside, told them I saw there was a problem, and asked them to try and work it out. First, they were taken off guard by the fact that I even perceived there to be difficulties since no one before really took the time to get involved in people situations. But they talked, and I listened. I offered advice and outlined the benefits to the company and to them personally of removing personnel hostilities. In less than four months, the barriers were down. I'm not saying the two are no longer competitive—I'm merely noting that the competition is a positive driving action in our organization."

Without a doubt, if someone lacks the basic technical ability to be a good people manager, he or she won't make it in a flat organizational environment. But I think another quality will prove even more important to success over the long run: being able to instill trust and cooperative attitudes. As we move into the new corporate culture, I am convinced that no one can successfully take a people leadership role without this ability.

To operate successfully in a flat, empowered organization, all employees who are your direct reports must believe that their future success will be dictated by what they do to create positive change in their area of responsibility. If they take the empowerment challenge seriously and try to network across the organization, they won't have much time to play politics up the organization to be sure they've got the right visibility and recognition. As a result, these individuals must have tremendous faith in you as their supervisor to take care of them. They must also be able to depend on you to give them access to additional resources if and when they need them to execute their empowered charter. This kind of relationship between you and your direct reports can't possibly occur unless the trust and cooperation between you are exceedingly strong. You must take the lead to create it.

If you end up with formal people management responsibilities in the new culture, engendering trust and cooperation will be a major part of your job. You'll need to enable employees to see career mobility opportunities. With less movement up the organization, people need prospects for horizontal mobility. Involvement in task forces that address businesswide issues is a perfect way for staff members to get meaningful exposure to new areas of the business.

Make a solid commitment to career development for all employees who seek it and are prepared to plunge their energies into it. Every employee should understand the value placed on the performance review as it relates to self-development. The review must be more than an annual measurement of rights and wrongs. Invest in your employees by giving them the knowledge and capabilities for a variety of roles in the company. The flat organization in no way constrains this developmental process, and managers should actively explore growth options for all employees in conjunction with the annual review.

There is no question in my mind regarding who the critical drivers will be as the transition accelerates between management cultures. Success will be dictated almost totally by middle managers and how they handle people management responsibilities. The emerging culture requires the reversal of many traditional value structures. The change can't happen without strong endorsement by senior management, but the execution depends on middle managers rebuilding the philosophies surrounding people management. None of the potential benefits of an empowered flatter organization structure will be realized if middle managers can't reorient the focus both at their peer level and in the staff below. You'll never be in a position to implement this cultural change unless you are trusted by peers and staff, and seen as someone who leads through cooperation and consensus rather than conflict and evasiveness. While you work on the people management skills so necessary to play a role in the change, go to work on any flaws that may exist in your reputation on these two core values.

I remember a manager telling me about a new concept one of his direct reports had for raising money for his company's annual United Way campaign. "I thought he was crazy. In our organization, this campaign holds so much importance that it's practically part of your performance review as a manager. The more your department contributes, the better your review. But this guy was fresh out of Management 101, and it was his first year for participating in the fundraising activities. And he'd inherited a department where trust wasn't any part of the department's vocabulary, especially in regard to this issue.

"However, this man wasn't to be deterred. He took a different approach instead of following our traditional method of holding one-on-one browbeating sessions that, by virtue of the subtle pressure, cause people to give more than they might otherwise be willing to contribute. He developed a sales campaign of sorts and held regular meetings, outlining where the money goes, who it helps, et cetera. And during these meetings, some of those lack-of-trust issues surfaced. No, he didn't get out a mallet. He said, 'Okay, I think you people will do the right thing and I'm not even going to review your contribution cards.' Shock. 'Simply turn them in inside an envelope and we'll see what we end up with.' I have to admit I was concerned, but as it turned out, the participation level was the highest ever for any group in my organization. His employees simply trusted his motives and recognized the integrity of his actions."

As you assess the challenges of people management in both a potential managerial role and as a more empowered employee within the organization, know that the factors for success will change with the shift in managerial cultures. "My specific accomplishments" will be much less important in the new culture in determining who rises to the top of the organization. "Our task force successfully solved a conflict between our organizations" will get much more applause and support from senior levels. People management and people influence skills will be of critical value for those with aspirations to lead a business.

I'm certainly not forecasting a complete reversal of the historic emphasis in performance evaluations on individual accomplishments. But there will certainly be an increased emphasis on the "softer" management skill of being a facilitator of constructive change in the company.

Rule 6: Make Your People Heroes

One of the toughest jobs anyone with people management responsibilities can have is keeping employees motivated. Some managers don't want to bother with this softer side to their management job because they can't see the connection to their bottom-line results. But I am convinced you can make a big difference to your company when you pay special attention to motivating and recognizing people for their contributions to the business.

There's no greater way to boost morale and improve overall performance than to demonstrate that you really care about what makes your people tick. Spend more personal time recognizing employees for a job well done; doing so invariably carries more motivational weight than a bonus check or a salary increase. Time and again, management surveys find that money is way down on the list of what keeps people satisfied in their jobs.

We've all had the experience of giving 110 percent to a project, only to have the boss ignore our efforts. The difference between no recognition at all and a pat on the back and a simple thank-you can make or break employees' attitudes about you, the company, and their jobs. And the smart manager knows that employees who excel can become role models for others in the business.

I doubt that what I'm saying is new to you. Most managers

know the essential facts about employee motivation, but too few of them capitalize on all the opportunities to build better morale. You can't benefit from better morale if you only work on building it when you happen to think of it. You have to prove through your actions, every day, that you honestly believe people are the most important asset in your organization. All that's required is ongoing recognition of your subordinates' accomplishments and the importance of their roles. Managers who truly understand the value of motivating employees do so constantly until it becomes a part of their operating style, even when maintaining motivation doesn't seem to be a relevant part of a particular job assignment.

One of my favorite examples of this kind of commitment from a manager is a high-level supervisor for a major communications company who was brought into a customer service operation of the business for six months with orders to shut it down. The business was to reopen later in another part of the country with a different staff, and the supervisor was charged with improving customer expectations while still smoothly winding down this particular unit.

This was a tough assignment for the supervisor: he had to handle a staff of employees who had always exhibited excessive absenteeism, and poor work habits and performance. They also knew they had nothing to gain or lose because they'd all be out of a job in six months. To add fuel to the inferno, the union was offering no support to management; its only concern was to shift blame for the closing onto management and away from the local union work rules that had made the location noncompetitive. Naturally, the employees didn't give a damn about assisting their new boss in upgrading the operation, but on the other hand, most managers wouldn't have worried much about morale under these circumstances. Most managers would have walked in, handed out marching orders, and left after completing the assignment. But not this manager.

"I knew I had my work cut out for me," he later told me, "so I pulled up every scrap of information I'd ever learned about managing people. The first thing I did was interview every one of the 50 employees in the organization. I wanted to learn what frustrated them, what motivated them, what they liked and didn't like about their jobs. In the process I learned a great deal about their personal lives as well. Most had received little recognition in their lives, whether from their home, school, or work environments. Many of them were dealing with tragic domestic situations, including substance abuse, which carried over into their work environment.

"It was clear that this was the first time any manager had taken the time to learn about them as people, not problems. I put myself in their shoes and thought about what it must be like never to get so much as a 'thanks'."

In his first month on the job, this supervisor made a point of rewarding everyone in some way. Banners on the walls proclaimed "We're a winning team," and buttons and ribbons with the same theme were distributed to emphasize that employees were going to turn the operation around by meeting the target he'd set for the six-month period.

The supervisor even drew and distributed caricatures of employees who had dealt particularly well with customer problems. He also created a collage of photographs of employees along with customer logos and pictures of the local baseball team, which had just won the regional championship—thus linking the employees' accomplishments to those of their local heroes. These items became the symbols of recognition for employees—something they had earned by doing an outstanding job. The supervisor also posted, in 10-inch lettering, goals and targets for the unit, as well as individual results. For the first time employees knew what their goals were and that their performance really mattered in keeping customers satisfied. Not only did they meet the supervisor's target, they surpassed it by 50 percent.

At this point, the supervisor vowed to find everyone a new assignment in the company, even though he knew he was going out on a limb with this type of promise. But he kept his word and placed all 50 employees; many even received promotions. In fact, the union actually worked with him to place people. Other units in the company came begging for these employees because they were now perceived as high achievers.

"It's tough to put into words just how much pride these people put into their jobs when they realized someone cared enough to recognize and appreciate them. I showed them that work could be fun and that their contributions actually made a difference to the business. This was probably the most satisfying management experience I've ever had, because I too felt an enormous sense of accomplishment for exceeding our plan."

This type of success story is becoming more common as managers experience the significant benefits of building employee recognition into their management styles.

I met the director of a large organization who went about creating a business culture that greatly differed from the corporation's traditional culture. Although what he established was not the complete opposite of the company's established culture, it certainly meandered from the corporate path. He told me how he introduced his own culture and leadership style and why it worked.

"The manager who preceded me fostered a lot of resentment in the staff, even about who might take his place. When I came on board, I could sense the mistrust. While our corporation pays a great deal of lip service to an open door policy, doors actually are closed. I began establishing my own values by having a real open door.

"Then I had to build the staff's confidence—show them I believed in their abilities—and encourage a team approach to improve the overall quality of our operation. I got blank stares in return. More often than not, our corporate culture dictated, 'Do the job and don't bug me.' But finally I began to make some headway. It was obvious that no one had ever taken the time to talk to these people—to get on the same wavelength.

"I conducted what I called quarterly meetings that began at 4:00 P.M. and called the first meeting to order by stating that its purpose was to thank everyone for doing a great job, that I really appreciated their efforts. More blank stares. They simply weren't accustomed to anyone recognizing their contributions. After about 15 minutes I announced, 'Let's have some pizza and beer.' They were completely thrown off guard. And although their workday ended at 4:40, they stayed at these meetings until 7:00— they were committing their own time.

"Although my leadership style continues to deviate from most of corporate management, I've been promoted several times because of it. I'll never forget, when I announced my promotion to another business in the company, a voice from the back of the auditorium inquiring, 'Does that mean the pizza parties are going to stop?' "

But turning people's attitudes around is not easy. It's an investment you have to make up front if you expect it to work. Once you do make such an investment, it can take time to get any return. Most employees have seen slogans and campaigns promoting the contributions they make come and go. If you want your efforts to have a real impact, you need to make people heroes while steadily earning their trust over time. Until they know you mean what you say, you won't see any change in their behavior.

When I first walked through the doors of Diners Club, I kept passing people who were on their way out—for good. Morale couldn't have been lower, and some of the best people were leaving because they believed management simply didn't care about them. One of my first business priorities was to change this perception. So I concentrated my efforts on a multitiered awards program for recognizing outstanding achievement. I wanted to make visible heroes of the people who went the extra mile for the company.

Throughout a two-year period, employees were recognized by their managers or peers for their performance as part of our Service Excellence Award program. Nonexempt winners of these awards became eligible for our most prestigious award, the FOCUS Award. Its broad purpose was to recognize an employee's

- Follow-through on the job
- Ownership perspective
- Customer sensitivity
- Being unsurpassed as a role model
- Service superiority

The winning prize was $25,000, an unprecedented award value for nonexempt employees, and one we chose to heighten the hero status we were placing on recipients.

The monetary value of the FOCUS Award, however, was not what made the biggest impact on the winner and the five runners-up. Much more significant was the visible way in which we recognized their contributions. We announced the award recipients at special ceremonies held in our two primary operating locations, with more than 2,000 Diners Club employees and their spouses in attendance. Celebrating the accomplishments of these six individuals did a great deal to legitimize our commitment to making heroes of our people in the organization. And I've seen and given enough after-dinner speeches to know that the six delivered on this occasion made a tremendous impact on the audience. When the winners spoke about what the award meant to them personally, the pride of each one was mirrored on the face of every employee there.

Throughout the FOCUS Award recognition process, we witnessed a turnaround in the business, especially in people's attitudes. I'm not suggesting that you need to award $25,000 if you want to recognize someone. I am proposing that you make a greater commitment to recognizing your employees' accomplishments. Usually without any monetary outlay, you'll find your own reward when you see the impact you have by creating heroes among your employees.

Maximizing Your People Relationship Credentials

We're in the early stages of the transition to the emerging management culture. If I were you, I would place the highest priority on developing people management skills, including the ability to influence associates across organizational lines when there is no direct reporting accountability. Acquire much broader and subtler skills than those required to manage direct-report relationships. Take a variety of training classes and courses on conversational techniques, listening skills, meeting process management, and any other area where people influence issues may arise.

Don't overlook the apprentice method for learning people management skills. Find managers with a reputation for excellent skills and figure out a way to become associated with them, not necessarily formally, so that you can learn some firsthand lessons. Find people who have worked for a model manager and pick their brains about what their boss did or didn't do in specific situations. Find out the war stories behind the model manager's reputation and try to incorporate their lessons into your own operating style.

The most important thing you can do to develop your people influence skills is to constantly practice them. No management skills come automatically, and personality is also a factor in establishing a working management style. You need to take conventional rules of management practice, adapt them to your personality, and then refine the resulting management skills so that they become second-nature to you in your working relationships.

A manager builds a reputation over time. Once it's established, people aren't easily persuaded that it's inaccurate. Be careful that yours doesn't reflect the cultural norm of winners and losers. If you expect to facilitate empowerment in your company, you have to become trusted. No one appreciates being clobbered by a corporate bully.

Traditionally, managers dealt with only a few people under their wings. They knew the jobs and the people doing them. While they typically became managers because they were the best at their particular functions, they often knew little about managing people. Why know more? It wasn't important for advancement in their own function.

All this is changing in the emerging culture. In a flattened organization, in which a people manager may have 15 direct reports, you can attain that level of responsibility only with exceptional people management skills. It doesn't matter what brilliant things you did before you took on the people management role—in the flattened organization, that role is now the most important part of your job.

4

The Second Key Experience: Building Customer Experiences

There is little controversy about at least one implication of the emerging culture for American corporations—meeting customer needs will be given higher priority. One primary reason is the increased domination of service companies, the growth engine for the U.S. economy in the 1990s. Service businesses simply can't afford any glitches in their procedures for accurately assessing customer needs and must position all their services to meet them. When service companies lose touch with their customers, they quickly become extinct.

Customer-driven priorities are reflected in many of the changes being felt by corporate America. Much of the motivation behind flatter organizational structures stems from corporate initiatives to put more people in closer contact with customers. Empowering employees is also justified largely by the customer-oriented benefits it provides. An empowered organization gives employees at all levels greater control over resources and greater authority to make decisions that satisfy customers at the moment of contact, when action is most needed—not hours or days later after the supervisory sign-off.

Companies will get religion about enhancing their customer orientation for many different reasons. All of them will lead to major opportunities for managers who can deliver new successes with customers. But you must first develop your customer management skills before you can use them to advance your career.

Marketing Experience Isn't an Automatic Win

One of the greatest misconceptions about customer management issues is that a marketing background is an automatic win. How often have you been told that marketing is your hot ticket to the executive suite? I'm always up for a good bet, but this isn't one of them. Look at the track record. Managers thumbing a ride out of marketing professions haven't left behind a library of new product success stories over the last ten years. In fact, corporate recruiters for senior management positions no longer place as high a premium on classic marketing backgrounds as they used to. What's really happening?

Based on my own experiences and on discussions with other senior executives and executive search professionals, the job market is cluttered with marketing professionals who simply don't have the credentials that corporations are looking for today. Most of their résumés highlight a set of skills that are suited only to executing a narrowly defined marketing function. Few ever demonstrate the ability to go eyeball to eyeball with a customer and make a difference that counts. The simple fact is that most marketers have never gotten their hands dirty in the trenches trying to establish customer relationships for the company. Don't be surprised when corporate management checks under your fingernails for signs of such efforts.

This new priority represents a major shift in how senior executives think about the marketing function and about the ability of marketing managers to handle the necessary work. They're beginning to realize that the marketing function is becoming too specialized to be a core skill that's really needed to compete in today's environment. Marketing professionals are expert at tracking data on purchase trends or analyzing sophisticated market research studies to tease out customer attitudinal variables that might produce market share changes. But the payoff for the investment in this research doesn't occur often enough. So senior management is coming to view all this sophisticated knowledge as a specialized staff function, not a valuable skill for reaping sales and profits.

Middle managers holding résumés that boast of their marketing genius are therefore just as vulnerable to the changes brought about by the emerging culture as those managers with other functional backgrounds. Cutbacks and consolidations in their companies are having drastic effects on their career opportunities and their functional areas. And these cutbacks aren't being compensated for with booming opportunity in other industries.

What Will It Take to Fill the Void?

Functional specialists won't make the grade in the 1990s. Instead, managers with a sixth sense about meeting customer needs will win the match. The manager's role isn't important; the right attitude is. Although marketing and sales managers could have an advantage in positioning their experience, they don't hold the automatic winning hand. The marketer who loves to play with numbers but avoids face-to-face customer contact will probably lose the game entirely. Similarly, the salesperson who pushes product on customers at all costs will also run out of cards.

Could it be that the largest emerging customer opportunity is in nontraditional functions like finance, production, and quality assurance? It's certainly true that flatter organizational structures give managers in these areas a chance to ask the relevant customer questions, to suggest the new directions that make sense in the long run, and to become the managers with the most credible customer focus when the new slots open up.

No matter what your current functional responsibilities are, you now have an opportunity to get onto center court and play the key match for your company team to win customers. Keep your eyes open for every move your company takes in a direction that contradicts a customer-driven philosophy. You'll never spot all of them in advance, but they're certain to crop up through your involvement in one business project or another. Recognize and grab these opportunities when you see them. In this chapter, I'll help you learn how to do that.

I've seen customer opportunities work both ways. Sometimes people step up to a situation to create a personal win and a company gain. At other times, a lack of leadership in customer responsibilities has pretty much buried a company's prospects for long-term growth.

Six Rules to Develop Customer Management Skills

The following six rules should help you shape and improve your own customer management style. To illustrate them, I'll also offer examples of how each one has been played out in a real business situation. Undoubtedly, your applications of these rules will be different, but I think the connections to your own experience will be clear.

As in chapter 3, I'd like you to complete a quick audit of your company's customer management orientation—again, to find out whether your company has a traditional 1980s culture or one more suited to the emerging 1990s culture. Score your company on the following 10 cultural characteristics, as you did in chapter 3.

Audit Your Company for Customer Management

Your Company	Traditional Culture	Emerging Culture
_____*	1. Sales and marketing staff are solely responsible for customer contact.	Staff from all departments are encouraged to spend time with customers whenever it makes sense.
_____	2. Employees view their boss as the only customer who really counts.	Employees confidently act on the principle that serving the paying customer takes precedence over other demands and job responsibilities.
_____	3. Customer complaints are handled by a special department with "canned" responses to various types of problems.	Handling customer complaints is everyone's priority, and even senior managers get personally involved in solving important customer problems.

*Score 0 point for Traditional Culture; 1 point for Emerging Culture

Traditional Culture	Emerging Culture	Your Company
4. A maximum budget is established for solving the problems of unhappy customers, and strict policies define what is allowable.	Staff are given great authority and latitude to do the right thing to solve each customer's problem in a timely fashion.	——
5. Customer attrition is not carefully analyzed or reported to senior management as a key business indicator.	Customer attrition is viewed as the most important measure of business health, and companywide resources are redirected immediately to solve any problem in this area.	——
6. Few dollars are spent on open-ended research into consumer needs and wants.	Significant ongoing investments are made in efforts to keep the business aware of what its customers really want.	——
7. The urgency to get a new product into the market is greatest when a competitor has already launched a similar product.	Launching a product that provides a unique breakthrough has a higher priority than keeping up with the competition.	——
8. The product ideas taken most seriously usually come from senior management.	Product ideas come from all over the organization and normally are triggered by someone's contact with customers.	——
9. When a senior manager drives a pet idea for a new product, he or she fends off any changes to the idea.	Regardless of the source of a new product idea, modifications to it are driven by customer rather than management reactions.	——
10. Promises to customers are invented and executed by the marketing and sales departments and the advertising agency, with no involvement from other functional areas.	Defining what to promise the customer and how to deliver it are viewed as the basic business strategy, and all key functions are involved in the process.	——

TOTAL

If your company's score is 8–10, you operate in a culture that positively supports your actions when you aggressively apply the six customer management rules, and your career will develop more rapidly than it would in a traditional culture. If the score is 4–7, you should apply these rules judiciously and look for opportunities to implement programs based on these rules. However, if the score is 0–3, you'll undoubtedly meet with a great deal of resistance because your actions will be out of synch with the company's cultural values. One advantage to operating in a traditional culture is that you'll have many opportunities to create visibility for yourself when you challenge the traditional wisdom. Just be sure you choose your test cases wisely.

Rule 1: Get Close to Your Customers—Know Who They Are and What They Want

Regardless of your functional position, get involved in any possible way with your customer base. There are enormous opportunities for face-to-face interaction, so be creative in your efforts. You'll be surprised at the measures you can take. If your responsibilities limit your direct customer involvement, read all the information you can get your hands on about the known behavior of your company's customers, from complaint letters to market research studies.

Above all, keep pushing the message that the customer's voice is the most important one in your organization. Safeguard that principle; never let the company walk away from it, and don't let misdirected research mask what your customers really want behind self-aggrandizing displays of what your company has to offer. If your aim is to help place the business on solid ground and move it forward, you can't base your views on biased data representing only the company's perspective.

Most of you know about companies that lost a business opportunity because their key decisions weren't driven by customer needs. A familiar example might be the company that introduces PCs with specially developed software into the education market. Perhaps you could even write the script for this one. The manager in charge of the project never gets a handle on who his customers are or what it is they really need. Instead, he focuses on the party holding the purse strings, the school administrators. Thinking they are the decision-makers, the manager completely overlooks his real customer: the teachers and students who will be using the equipment.

The problem is almost always compounded because of this basic flaw in customer focus. The sale is made, and PCs begin to arrive at the schools. It isn't long before teachers are pulling out their hair over the actual software application and overall design failures. They identify their concerns in the warranty cards that they promptly return to the PC company. The cards, of course, go to the quality control area, where employees look only at equipment function issues.

Because school administrators are still ordering the PCs, the positive financial message is masking the message from the real customer. It's right in front of the company's nose on the warranty cards, but no one takes the time to read them. The message couldn't be clearer: almost all teachers who got the PCs rejected the software because it doesn't work in the classroom. They don't have an equipment function problem, they have an applications problem. To the teachers, there is no difference; the PCs simply don't deliver. No area of the company sees this as a problem as long as the orders keep coming from the school administrators. But eventually the real customer has the final say, and the product is returned because it doesn't work. The real customer almost always has the last word. The lesson in all this: give them the *first* word.

There's plenty of literature about the companies that bought the farm because they couldn't sell a product that didn't meet customer needs. Had the PC company manager broadened his functional perspective, had he identified the actual customer up front, I might be telling you a success story instead of one about a sorry failure.

You can, however, read about some successes. A manager with a large publishing house recalled how working directly with a customer to develop a new program realized tremendous rewards—and profits. "A few of us had considered electronic printing of books for several years, but the concept was foreign to many and a lot of people didn't share our enthusiasm. Then we had a particular opportunity to work with a customer who wanted to customize books electronically, on demand, in small quantities. This was a revolutionary idea in book publishing.

"To take advantage of it, we formed a small task force that spent a great deal of time with the outside customer, the ultimate customer, who would use the product. This allowed us to identify every element of what our customers were looking for in electronic production, from a customer perspective. I don't think there is a better way to know what our customers want than to work with them, first-hand. We gained tremendous insight into their own values and culture. Moreover, we used the successful experience with this customer as an example for other business groups in the company."

Another manager I know told me how she recognized an opportunity to upgrade the customer service in her organization. Initially, there was ongoing skepticism and miscommunication between her marketing area and the customer service division. This lack of unity was understandable in part because so many of the staff were new to the company. "But it became apparent," she told me, "that the managers in my department wanted it to be autonomous—they didn't want anyone else involved in what we do. So there was little working together from a customer standpoint.

"The customer service department was getting a lot of calls about our marketing programs, and were trying to get some cooperation on how to handle certain issues. Instead, they got nothing. The longer this situation prevailed, the more the resentment between the two groups intensified.

"Because I previously worked for a much smaller company in which everybody was concerned about the customer, it was difficult for me to understand why no one was asking the customer service department what was wrong, and why we were fighting with them. So I scheduled an appointment with my peer in that department, and we spoke openly about specific actions we could take to resolve our differences and to improve customer satisfaction. As a start, we offered training sessions to customer service personnel about our new products.

"Then, we had both departments visit our outside order-processing facility to meet the people we constantly interface with and see their operation. We set up an online system so that when customers called, our representatives could instantly see what was going on with their orders. Finally, we had customer service become more involved in our telemarketing activities, which are very sensitive from a customer service standpoint—for example, they review our vendors' scripts before we ever use them.

"Overall, we've become more sensitive to the departments that directly interface with our customers, showing them exactly what we do that affects the customers. This also smooths our internal operations. But the bottom line is that customer satisfaction is at its highest level in our area because we acted on what people were telling us about how to benefit our customers."

The customer services division of a major Midwest computer company is working at better understanding customer needs; its nationwide operating principle is, "Think like a customer." Division employees pin the button carrying this credo on their shirts, confident that they're actually practicing what they preach—servicing customers from a customer rather than a company perspective.

If opportunities for direct, or even indirect, customer involvement arise in your job, seize them. Even consider taking a lateral move or a step down in position temporarily to help establish your credibility in speaking for the customer in all your actions.

Rule 2: Don't Filter What Customers Tell You— Even When It Hurts to Hear It

If you've never had firsthand experience with the collection and interpretation of data about customer behavior, this rule might seem perplexing at first. I'm not suggesting that marketers "cook the books" in the sense of purposefully manipulating marketing data. But anyone who has observed market research processes knows that many subjective judgments go into data collection and reporting.

I cringe when market research experts boast about their ability to create "totally objective" research studies. In fact, consumer research questionnaires can be very subtly slanted to produce results diametrically opposite to what's really going on in the marketplace. There's simply much less precision in market measurements than you'll find in financial or operating data collection on internal company performance.

It's not difficult to see that if the messenger is shot for delivering bad news to senior executives, the messenger will prefer to give the news that gets a better reaction. For most senior executives, bad news is data that refute their strategy decisions. But a vicious cycle is set in motion when the objective realities of the customer marketplace are masked by a process that reinforces erroneous news, however well it supports the business strategy. Delivering only "good" news looks like a safe decision at first glance, but things have a way of catching up. And the pain and trauma can be enormous when managers take action based on a biased and inaccurate understanding of the customer.

I confronted such a dilemma when I consulted for Scott Paper some years ago. Scott always struggled to overcome the patent-protected advantage of its rival Kleenex, namely, tissues that pop up out of the box one at a time. For years Scott management was convinced that the company's inability to re-create this feature was the major barrier to its penetration of Kleenex's market.

In the early 1970s Scott's engineers finally devised a new box design with such a feature. Because of the significant capital investment that had to be made to convert to the new design, market research was conducted to determine customer attitudes about the new feature. The results confirmed management's beliefs, and the change was made at a lightning pace.

As soon as the new tissue-box feature was introduced, complaints began to roll into Scott from customers who preferred a box from which a handful of tissues could be grabbed. Management was already committed to the change, so they convinced themselves that this reaction represented only a small group of customers. Sales, however, supported the customers' reactions, not management's.

When, several years later, Scott found itself in a profit squeeze, the word went out to the company's operating divisions to seek cost-saving opportunities. The engineering group proposed removing the box's cardboard liner that gave it the pop-up feature. The savings would be impressive, but management asked for further market research to determine customer attitudes about the change.

Not surprising, management's desire to eliminate the feature and save money was supported by the research, which found that people really didn't care much about pop-up tissues. The change was instituted, the cost savings were achieved, and another round of complaint letters arrived from a different group of Scott customers.

Telling this story in several paragraphs instead of the several years' time it actually took to occur leaves an obvious message that was less apparent in real life. The problem was not with the marketing opportunities but with the management decision-making process. By researching customer preferences before it acted, Scott seemed to be taking all the right steps. But if you examine the design of the research, you'll discover that its results were predetermined.

A manager with a large utility company faced a similar challenge. "In serving the residence market, everyone is supposedly an expert—we all have telephones. So while we always get a lot of customer feedback, it isn't always taken advantage of.

"We were in the process of developing a program that top management was convinced our customers were going to love. But those of us who work very closely with our customers on a daily basis thought otherwise. We had direct evidence that customer reactions would differ greatly from management's expectations. Sure enough, when the program was implemented, the initial response was negative. Customers saw all kinds of hidden motives for what we were trying to do, and, in fact, thought we were stepping away from our service commitment rather than enhancing it. Naturally, I was concerned because I didn't see the data balancing between customer and management expectations. But management still has a halo around the concept and continues to invest in seeing it through."

When the predispositions of senior management are well understood by the organization, there is internal pressure to create results that support them. These biases are seldom conscious, but they are very real. It's tremendously dangerous to take action believing that objective support from management exists when, in fact, it does not.

Seeking new customer data from every possible source is a valuable way to overcome the biases we all have. Aggressively look for data that both confirm *and* refute your assumptions about what customers want. This data will help you control your natural biases. When you're scrutinizing data from the marketplace for factuality, dig deep to uncover subjective biases. You can never lose in the long run by driving for the truth. Data that refute our biases are often more important than those that confirm them.

This assertion isn't as farfetched as it sounds. When I consulted for Anheuser-Busch on the company's advertising effectiveness, market tests revealed that sales decreased when more advertising dollars were spent. This result was completely counterintuitive, and to the Anheuser-Busch advertising agency, completely ridiculous. The advertising agency decided that the test had given false readings. I didn't buy that explanation and pursued one that better fit the facts.

I discovered that customers reached a turnoff point when they were bombarded by particular advertising messages. Anheuser-Busch could stretch millions of advertising dollars by learning how to spot these turnoff points. Such data can refine your view of the customer and enable you to set better business strategies.

At first you might be tempted to blame customer irrationality for behavioral data that don't conform to your presumptions. You find yourself asking how that uninformed customer could possibly know more than you about your business. Don't fall into that trap. I have found that customers know precisely what they want and why they want it. If you challenge this knowledge, you simply don't understand your customers. Constantly seek that understanding rather than fling around unfounded accusations of irrationality.

I bumped into this attitude at Campbell while working on a new shape for a plastic beverage container to replace our large-sized juice can. Initially, our designs were round, similar to the two-liter soft-drink bottle. Customers liked the plastic bottle's lightness, but not its shape. Then we produced a rounded, rectangular container with flat sides on the label area. Customers loved it, but we thought their response was an irrational attraction to a new look—until we started listening more closely. They told us that the new shape fit neatly in the refrigerator door, whereas the soft-drink bottle merely added to the container clutter on the top shelf.

While you are trying to understand customer behavior and looking for information to support it, become the customer's voice in your organization, whatever your functional responsibilities. Often the greatest benefits of understanding customers accrue to managers whose responsibilities don't normally include making assessments of customer behavior. They can freely think about business implications on an overview basis because they don't live with the details day-to-day. The more refined your understanding, the better your position in the emerging customer-driven culture.

Rule 3: Treat Every Dissatisfied Customer as a Threat to Business Survival

Common sense says that a company should worry about losing dissatisfied customers. Most American corporations, however, have always tried harder to add to their customer base than to retain existing customers. Just look at the rewards and incentives your company provides its sales force. If your company is like most, it is almost totally driven by efforts to attract new customers. That's fine if you also reward efforts to retain customers. Can you identify such an effort in your company, and does it get the same level of visibility as the effort to create new business? In almost all companies, the answer is a resounding no.

There are real opportunities to increase awareness in your organization about the dissatisfied customers who want out, but no one wants to talk about them. However unpleasant, that discussion is absolutely essential if the company is going to win in the marketplace. Look for opportunities to open your company's ears to what its customers are saying. Johnson & Johnson listened, even when the going was smooth.

I remember reviewing market research studies that Johnson & Johnson completed on its Tylenol brand of pain reliever. Tylenol's sales were just taking off, and the product was gaining a reputation as a safe alternative to aspirin. Since the safety issue was important to consumers at that time, the company had a hit on its hands.

But the market research on Tylenol pinpointed a potential problem amid the good news. Many consumers didn't believe the product was as effective as aspirin. That belief wasn't supported medically, but consumers assumed that a safer product must be a weaker one and that they still needed a strong analgesic to knock out their splitting headaches. Seeing this as pure opportunity, Johnson & Johnson introduced Tylenol Extra Strength, which was immediately successful and helped the company to expand a brand success. Johnson & Johnson executives were committed to listening to customers—even when everything was going well.

Johnson & Johnson analyzed and addressed customer concerns that could have threatened acceptance of its product. Many other companies, however, use customer research to camouflage decisions they've already made. What an enormous waste of effort—not just in the collecting of biased but useless information but also in the making of important decisions with absolutely no basic knowledge about customer behavior.

Many companies tend to use advertising to tell customers what the company thinks should be important to them without asking them first. For years American corporations have paid lip service to the idea that "the customer is always right." But they are only now backing up that idea with strategic substance. Still, there have always been a few mavericks willing to buck the system and establish a new set of standards. One such pioneer was Stew Leonard, who opened a single-store dairy in Connecticut. What a success story his business has become since that time! But the roots of this particular success were actually planted when Leonard made the commitment to walk the aisles of his store and interact with his customers.

The visible success of Stew Leonard's customer philosophy caught the attention of more than a few interested spectators. In *Thriving on Chaos,* Tom Peters discusses Leonard's ability to get people turned on to service. For example, Leonard figured that whenever he saw a frown on the face of a customer, he was looking at $50,000 walking out of his life forever. His logic was flawless. Leonard calculated that his average customer patronized his store for about ten years, and that during that time the customer bought around $100 worth of groceries per week, 50 weeks a year. Multiply those three numbers and you come up with Leonard's value for each customer—$50,000.

My own attempt to make sure "the customer is always right" at Diners Club in the late 1980s resulted in the first big breakthrough in our bad-debt collection area. When cardholders got so behind in their payments that they were turned over to our collections group, they were managed there as a problem account rather than as customers in need of service. We wanted our money and were prepared to sever the customer relationship entirely if that was the only way to collect it. Unfortunately, some of our customers who ended up being handled by the collections group actually had disputes about merchant payments. When we talked to them about their delinquent accounts, we largely discounted their pleas about billing disputes as another delaying tactic to avoid payment. As a result, we lost some good customers.

We solved the problem when we instituted a new management unit that treated early payment delinquencies as a customer service issue. In other words, we gave the customers the benefit of the doubt until we could prove otherwise. Only then did they become a collections problem. This change in attitude not only improved our handling of billing disputes, it produced solid results on legitimate collection problems.

Diners Club started focusing on customer retention in other ways as well. One significant action was eliminating limits on the length of time a customer service representative could spend on the phone. Prior to that change, our managers were so focused on quantitative efficiency standards that they would reprimand representatives who spent too much time with a customer. Such pressure kept our representatives from delivering quality service. One of the earliest such efforts to empower reps was made by a major insurance company, which installed mirrors in front of each customer service representative with the printed reminder, "Even though customers can't see you, they can feel your facial expression. Smile."

It isn't difficult to improve customer satisfaction. Just listen to what customers tell you and follow their marching orders. It is much more difficult to improve a company's customer awareness. But the important first step is making the development of that awareness a top priority. I suggest you take the initiative in doing so today.

Rule 4: Don't Turn Down Opportunities Because "It's Not Our Business"

Think big, act small. When companies gain a secure market position, they're more likely to discount customer preferences with rationales like, "Interesting, but that's not our business." This is a paralyzing, sometimes lethal, attitude.

Always challenge the company's product or service ground rules when you're exposed to customer desires that seem to conflict with them. If customer preferences are legitimate, they're a business opportunity waiting for someone to exploit. Face it, if a competitor grabs hold of that opportunity, how will your company feel about its own conservatism? Senior executives are going to notice the manager who talked the company into being the first to grab an unorthodox but profitable opportunity.

During my own business endeavors a decade ago, certain proposals were categorically turned down because "it is not our business." I was often on the receiving end of that credo, particularly during a consulting project for Columbia Pictures that involved a broad charter to help the company better understand why a movie audience reacts favorably to one picture and not another. The focus was on identifying particular appeals to segments of the moviegoing population.

In the course of our project, we encountered an interesting study in which movie audiences had been surveyed after viewing a movie with a comedy theme. Unknown to the audience, a staged group attended the previous showing. When the staged group came out of the theater laughing and joking about the film, the surveyed audience that followed also expressed considerable pleasure with the film. But when the staged group left the theater frowning and grousing about what a terrible movie they'd just seen, the surveyed audience reported a similar level of dissatisfaction.

This suggested to us that perhaps satisfaction was related to some extent to how well the audience was set up to enjoy the movie. We decided to test the idea that audiences needed to be prepped with something like a warm-up act.

We took a movie that Columbia was about to release that the experts believed would be a marginal success at best. To test the warm-up concept, we created a 10-minute film to present before the movie in selected theaters across the country. Audiences were asked to rate the feature film, and their ratings did indeed indicate more positive reactions when the warm-up film was shown beforehand. Since neither film produced outstanding audience reactions, however, the film producer and director, frustrated with having a loser on their hands, attacked the test for "screwing up their audiences." Thus, the test was halted. The idea that audience reaction to a movie could be influenced by factors other than the movie itself was simply too radical for movie professionals. The movie business remains narrowly focused to this day.

I ran into a similar barrier when I served as vice president of Marketing and Business Development for the Swanson Foods Division of Campbell Soup. Customers considered our Swanson frozen dinners to be very good for frozen food, but a far cry from homemade. The gap simply couldn't be explained by the data on the actual food quality. Turkey dinners, one of Swanson's leading sellers, took a particularly hard hit in customer ratings.

One of the well-known characteristics of food quality perceptions is that food aroma is a more significant factor than actual taste. Was it possible, we pondered, that this tendency applied to frozen foods more than we'd realized? Further analysis of the reaction to our turkey dinners confirmed this notion. Although a Swanson frozen dinner could be close to the quality of a home-made turkey dinner, the kitchen aroma of a turkey roasting in the oven all day could not be compared to that of one of our frozen turkey dinners being heated up. In fact, our dinners had virtually no aroma as they cooked.

This realization led to some interesting strategic thinking. Since we were converting our packaging from aluminum trays to paper and plastic containers, we started looking for a way to artificially enhance the aroma of the food while it cooked. The idea was to impregnate the bottom of the container with food aroma capsules that would be released as the oven temperature increased, with no contamination of the food. If the perceived quality of the product could be substantially enhanced as a result, was this not a marketing strategy that should be pursued?

Although the project was extensively discussed, the company's resources remained more focused on the product than on the total delivery system. Defining what creates value in the minds of customers was not pursued any further, and the project never made it to the playing field.

But some companies, mostly smaller ones, have brilliantly redefined their business. A friend of mine, Bob Hanke, is a good example of this kind of innovation. Bob was a new MBA graduate from Wharton, and he was anything but typical. With a Ph.D. in theoretical physics, a field he worked in for several years with a large corporation, Bob came across an opportunity he couldn't pass up.

PCs hadn't yet made their impact on the business market in the mid-1970s, but the earlier generations of online computer terminals with substantially improved model-building software were already emerging. Bob began a software development and business consulting company to capitalize on the market situation.

Computer terminals were essentially IBM Selectric typewriters with the famous round type ball. For different applications, the equipment operator changed the type ball in the machine. One afternoon while working on a software program, Bob dropped a type ball and a tooth that held the ball in the typewriter broke. Although the replacement cost was less than $100, it was more than he could afford.

Bob spent most of the afternoon attempting to repair the ball and finally succeeded. For just about anyone else, this would have been the end of the story. But Bob took his idea to a friend, and the two of them worked out a relatively simple system for making permanent repairs on broken IBM Selectric type balls.

The national market for this service was larger than anyone realized. Since IBM had a captive market for new type balls to replace the broken ones, it had no interest in providing repair service. Consequently, almost every corporation threw the type balls away. Bob's repair business realized attractive margins and grew to substantial size with product diversifications before he eventually sold it for a handsome profit.

Besides his ability to spot and capitalize on a customer opportunity, Bob had another management characteristic common to entrepreneurs who use those opportunities to shape their businesses. He had perfect timing on when to sell a business—in this case, just when the Selectric typewriter was at its peak. New technologies began to emerge soon thereafter, and the group that bought Bob's company found itself in a declining maintenance market. Bob, on the other hand, invested his profits from the sale of his business in an entirely new business direction that has proven to be even more successful than his type ball repair business.

A successful long-range business strategy is a delicate balance between delivering the best products or services and delivering the ones customers really want. Often, managers in the best position to react to customer preferences are those with little or no responsibility for the company's existing offerings. With a little effort, could you be the one to lead your company in making a better response to customer requests—a response that could lay the foundation for a new business approach?

Rule 5: Give Your Customers Guarantees of High Performance—and Put Them in Writing

Companies historically have tended to get some of the basic marketing principles backward. Particularly annoying is the practice of using market research not to identify weaknesses and devise solutions, but rather to produce, at great expense, advertising slogans that suggest those weaknesses don't exist. We've destroyed plenty of advertising investments this way. Somehow we think we can fool the customer by making promises about what we'd like our company to be. Customers will believe us for a while—until we don't deliver on the promise.

A new strategy is emerging to overcome the skepticism customers have developed toward advertising slogans. No-strings-attached guarantees are a hot new marketing topic. Naturally, customers are responding, and guarantees are now shaking up the marketing approaches of many businesses.

A small number of innovative companies during the 1980s first saw the powerful potential of service guarantees. Guarantees weren't just a marketing gadget for them, but a way to improve service delivery itself. They felt that the lost revenue from not meeting some guarantees was a small price to pay for the valuable data the guarantees would provide on service weaknesses. By contrast, most businesses don't want to see their problems with customer satisfaction become highly visible in the company. As a result, they shrink from making guarantees but risk alienating customers.

Organizations like Nordstrom Department Stores and Domino's Pizza are responsible for putting the guarantee concept on the map. They made guarantees so enticing to customers that they captured every unsatisfactory delivery in their customer base. I remember when I first heard about Tom Monaghan's innovative service ideas for Domino's back in 1960. For more than 30 years now, delivery of a Domino's order to a customer's door cannot take longer than 30 minutes; if it does, the customer pays nothing. Even if delivery takes 31 minutes, Domino's foots the bill.

Monaghan's employees, or "Dominoids," pay close attention to the customer because the company has always pegged their salaries to customer satisfaction. And the company pays 10,000 mystery customers $60 each to purchase a dozen pizzas throughout the year in locations nationwide to evaluate quality and service. Monaghan partly bases his managers' salaries on those evaluations. In fact, Domino's regional offices regularly rate the quality of the service they're receiving from headquarters, and the stores rate the distribution companies that supply ingredients. Similarly, employees who measure up are apt to find themselves a few bucks richer around bonus time. As we now know, this passion for service quality enabled Domino's and similar businesses to continually improve on their products and services. Today, these organizations aren't worried about who's trying to catch up to them; they're too far ahead, and deservedly so.

At Diners Club we offered a guarantee to our customers in

relation to managing corporate travel and entertainment expenses that required throwing the ground rules out the window. Few executives realize that travel and entertainment (T&E) expenses are their third-largest controllable expense. Because such expenses are disbursed throughout the organization, no one realizes the magnitude of the dollars. Equally, no one tries to coordinate the management of T&E expenses to gain savings.

Both Diners Club and American Express went to work on creating corporate awareness of the opportunity to manage T&E expenses. Since no one in most companies has this responsibility, gaining an audience was difficult. So both card companies focused on a single, tangible issue—cash management—that could be solved through a corporate credit card. Dollar benefits for a corporate card program were clearly established because companies paid for T&E expenses on corporate credit cards much later than through normal billing processes.

The cash management savings worked to get the ball rolling on corporate card programs but were only the tip of the potential iceberg. There were far greater savings to be made from a total T&E management system that would, for instance, define travel policies for employees, negotiate discounts from travel suppliers, and design cost-efficient expense-reporting systems. A good corporate card system could facilitate all this, to the benefit of everyone concerned. Only one roadblock remained: getting corporate attention at the target companies focused on this opportunity.

During one of our brainstorming sessions with the sales force, someone proposed a solution that changed all the ground rules. Instead of trying to sell a corporation on the concept and then delivering the promised gains after the sale, why not offer up front a risk-free guarantee of savings? To carry out the strategy, Diners Club would have to take the risk for achieving the savings, as well as manage the implementation of the system. In exchange for the risk, we would take our profits from savings achieved above the guarantee level. Because corporations paid so little attention to T&E expenses, they had no basis on which to reliably estimate the actual gains that could be realized by managing the system as a whole. Our solution looked like windfall profits to them.

Guarantees of performance standards will continue to be a

viable marketing concept as long as companies make sure they're formulated from a customer perspective. If you get the chance to formulate or implement guarantees, see that they incorporate the customer's interests above all else.

Rule 6: Preach the Gospel of Customer Satisfaction Whether Your Customers Are Inside or Outside the Company

Some people would argue that acceptable financial performance is the lifeblood of a company's success. This perspective is changing as it sinks in with corporate America that healthy profits are a consequence rather than the cause of a company's success. Good financial numbers can't be manufactured out of thin air. Financial success begins with good customer relationships, which create the revenue stream that supports, and justifies investments in, the business.

Although more and more senior executives are claiming that customer satisfaction is their company's top priority, they're not always matching their actions to that credo. It's so easy to forget the customer satisfaction priority in the daily rush of management tasks. Many departments in a business seldom, if ever, have the chance to listen directly to customers. It's no wonder that the priority can lose its edge, even though it remains a solid basis for everyone's actions.

You can help your organization by making customer satisfaction a second-nature priority in all your own management actions. By heightening your own sensitivity to the issue, you can begin to challenge those company activities that have no link to customer benefits. Your internal alarm about actions which lack customer relevancy will undoubtedly go off more times than you're able to act on. Even with your consciousness of customers raised, you'll be surprised at how few of your own projects are really aimed at strengthening customer satisfaction. You'll also find that even people in functions that offer direct customer contact won't have a very high batting average when it comes to making customer satisfaction a priority. That fact is a reflection of how easily business organizations can let their energies be diverted from their mission.

Because few functional areas have direct contact with a company's customers, customer satisfaction is often discharged indirectly by serving the employees who are directly responsible for making customers happy. These internal "customers" become the conduit to the external customer.

Treat internal customers the same way you'd treat external ones. What products and services do they expect you to provide? Have you spent time listening to their needs and wants? Do you know what they think of the products you're providing today? How do you measure the cost justification for your actions to deliver products to those customers? Most companies ask these questions all the time about external customers but don't apply them to their own employees when services are designed for them. That's a mistake you can correct by leading the charge to give your internal customers equal time and attention.

If you're willing to let internal customer demands drive your department's activities, you could find yourself making sweeping changes in what you do and how you do it. But you must start with the fundamentals; that is, you have to find out what your customers really want from you. When you feel you have a reasonably accurate profile of your internal customers' needs, have the guts to make changes as radical as necessary to support those needs. If your internal products and services aren't doing the job for your customer base, you're extremely vulnerable. It's only a matter of time until your customers begin to walk away. If they can't leave because they're forced to use you as their supplier, you can bet they'll constantly complain to the world about your area's incompetence. Don't wait for the inevitable crisis caused by a dissatisfied customer. Fix the problem now.

When both internal and external customers are being satisfied, every segment of the business becomes seriously focused on providing satisfaction to some customer group. And if internal customers who directly serve one another keep their perspective on the ultimate external customer as king, they will begin to reposition their activities to have a more direct impact on meeting the needs of the ultimate customers—the most meaningful constituency any business group can have. Barring that possibility, they'll redirect their efforts toward those internal customers who are clearly meeting the needs of external customers. The last party any functional area will want to service is an internal customer group that is unable to have an impact on the external customer.

There's no better way to stamp out the care and feeding of irrelevant internal bureaucracies than to get all functional areas accustomed to making customer satisfaction a priority. The word gets out fast: if you're not serving the customer, you'd better be serving an internal group that is.

At Diners Club all functional areas survey our internal customers to determine their satisfaction with the various services provided. From these results, each area uses a set of planned service adjustments to improve satisfaction. The smallest change, such as making sure phone calls are returned promptly, can bring enormous results. Some functions in the business, such as training activities in our service organization, have become so customer-focused that they have considered splitting off to become profit rather than cost centers. More power to them!

NCR chairman Chuck Exley has made great strides in building internal customer relationships through his company's "stakeholder" philosophy. Stakeholders are any individuals—employees, shareholders, suppliers, members of the community—with a stake in the company's growth. The premise is that all internal customers have an equal stake in the company's prosperity and must treat one another accordingly. Thus, tremendous value is placed on internal customer relationships that cross over various functional territories.

NCR's stakeholder philosophy is further supported through healthy decentralization that allows individual functions to operate as profit centers. Within each unit, internal and external customers are given equal treatment. The rationale is that services that are good enough for one should be good enough for the other. Subsequently, NCR's internal customers pay for services they obtain from other departments, just like any external customer.

A word of caution. Companies get themselves into trouble by pricing themselves out of the internal market. If a product or service passes through too many hands, the end-user could often have made a better deal outside. When all the price hand-offs take place and everyone involved gets a fair margin, the final internal customer may be stuck with an inflated bill. The only way to maintain workable internal customer relationships is to allow these customers to abandon internal suppliers demanding inflated prices just as an external customer can.

You have an enormous opportunity to practice what you preach by taking your internal customers seriously. Your company might not be as far out in front of this issue as a company like NCR, with its stakeholder philosophy. But your own credibility as a customer-driven manager will be strengthened if you manage from this priority, and you'll accumulate tangible accomplishments that, on your résumé, will demonstrate an ability to make a difference to customers. No functional area has a lock on this mission.

A manager I know was responsible for technical education and had to answer questions about the value of and justification for educating employees. The function was perceived by users—that is, internal customers—as a system forced on the organization. "There was a general lack of understanding of the importance of good internal and external relationships within the company," he noted. "While ours was an extremely professional and capable group, we didn't have much of a relationship with our customers. I was determined to convince our internal customers—all company employees who service our external customers—that we were there to improve service, not waste their time.

"We stressed over and over that the field needed the education for education's sake and not because 'the home office said so' or because we were trying to drive revenues by their participation. The process took 18 months, but in the end, the field organization perceived our focus to be exactly what we'd been saying it was. We increased participation by 20,000 student-days. The field organization still had a financial commitment because they were paying for all the expenses of this education, but their support signaled the beginning of a cooperative effort on the part of both groups."

Maximizing Your Customer Credentials

I cannot emphasize enough the importance of orienting yourself to customer needs and demands. Look at the movers and shakers in this decade and you'll find customer orientation underlying their success. I seriously doubt that you want your business to lag behind, with you personally tailing even further behind. But achieving the right customer orientation isn't easy. Good intentions alone will not move your strategy forward. It's all too easy for companies to assume they are supporting the same values they attribute to their customers. But as a company begins to place too much importance on the products or services it offers, it often becomes blinded to what drives consumer purchasing decisions. Make sure that doesn't happen to you.

5

The Third Key Experience: Building Leadership Credentials

Leadership has received a lot of press in the past decade. But in spite of the many new definitions of leadership in the literature, there apparently has been a lack of the real thing. Corporate America has witnessed the burial of companies run by individuals who possessed neither the vision nor the acumen to guide their businesses through trying economic and competitive times. Building their reputations almost exclusively on administrative abilities, traditional senior managers haven't fostered the growth necessary to keep pace in the global marketplace.

The leadership issue still rages, and in the emerging management culture the focus won't be restricted to senior managers. Leadership credentials will be demanded of managers in every functional area, and the new leaders will be required to create an organizational vision that encompasses all the emerging trends—more emphasis on people relationships, empowering employees to act on behalf of the business and its customers, strong communication skills, and the ability to support all the company's functional elements to benefit the business as a whole.

In their book *Leaders* (1985), Warren Bennis and Burt Nanus outline the credentials that effective corporate leaders of the future will need to have. You might consider the four leadership attributes they discuss as you assess your own qualifications. *Vision* is at the top of their list—the ability to define a realistic and desirable state the organization should attain at some future date. Second is *communication,* which includes a leader's ability to describe his or her vision to others in such a way that they're inspired to participate in it, to assume ownership. *Positioning* is an attribute of leaders who can make the pieces of their organization work together consistently and harmoniously to bring their visions to life. Finally, Bennis and Nanus identify *self-management* as a necessary leadership characteristic—the ability to build an environment in which people have the freedom to unleash their creativity in specific actions.

If your long-range goal is to run your own business (a desire of some but by no means everyone), you should read Bennis and Nanus, among others, on business leadership.

What Is Leadership?

In discussing leadership, I'll be taking a different tack from what you might expect. I feel strongly that leadership and its attendant skills encompass far more than a specific talent for heading up a business. There are leadership qualifications you should develop even if you never leave the middle management ranks. We usually think of leadership as that particular set of skills acquired by those who reach the top. I see this assumption changing, however, as the foundation of bureaucratic and hierarchical businesses crumbles.

My ideas about leadership in the emerging culture parallel those I've discussed about people management. Today people management skills are generally associated only with those managers with direct-report responsibilities. But flatter organizations and broader empowerment are going to demand people management skills of every manager. Without a doubt, there will continue to be traditional development needs in the future for those who will have direct report relationships. But people management skills will broaden and change for all managers. One caution: people management will be a dangerous term through the transition period of management cultures because it's so likely to take on a stereotyped, narrow meaning.

The same can be said about leadership. In the coming decade we'll need broader leadership abilities from managers at all levels, not just from the people running the business. The same cultural forces of change that are causing people management abilities to spread throughout organizations are also behind the spread of a new brand of leadership in most businesses.

Flatter structures and empowered employees require managers at every level to have detailed and in-depth knowledge beyond their own area of responsibility. They'll need to integrate that knowledge with input from other managers to establish "right" solutions for the business. Just what are those right solutions? In my view, they'll be the various answers to one simple question: "If I owned the entire business, how would I want the decision to be shaped?"

The leadership characteristics that Bennis and Nanus describe can be integrated with the characteristics I'll discuss in this chapter. These leadership characteristics have somewhat different applications at job levels other than top management. But once we make the appropriate adjustments, how to apply them to your personal development program will become obvious.

Middle Manager Leadership

Middle managers confront leadership challenges every day; they just don't get the same press as the CEO who makes a courageous move to better position the whole company. Not long ago at Diners Club, we were fighting an extremely tight deadline to release a major new product enhancement into the marketplace. Every day we delayed our launch further compromised our chances of capitalizing on the competitive advantages we believed we had. A complicated redesign of our computer system was necessary before we could implement the marketing program; the systems analysts looked at the project requirements and gave us an estimate of the labor and time involved in such a redesign. Our internal auditors looked at the checks-and-balances procedures we needed to take and then added more time to the project. Then additional time was added for servicing the new product. When we added up the time investment, our market opportunity evaporated.

Almost everyone involved was frustrated with the schedule but accepted the timetables as "what it takes to implement complex new programs." But one manager just couldn't swallow it. She had enough background in all the functional pieces of the planning schedule to see the alternative actions that would dramatically shorten the schedule. As she aired her ideas, the groups whose schedules she was challenging rose in resistance. Failure would have grave consequences for the business, they all intoned. But this manager didn't back off.

After weighing the consequences of adopting a risky new process that could meet the schedule against missing the deadline for the product launch, we opted for the manager's plan. She established an implementation team from across the business, ran the project from a central "war room," and met every deadline she'd set. Frankly, I think she succeeded because every member of the team knew how far she had stuck her neck out to deliver the product for our marketing group. When the project was successfully completed, we publicized her achievement to the rest of the business. One purpose in spreading the news was to show everyone not just the leadership potential in the situation but how one person successfully took on a leadership challenge.

I feel that leadership isn't exhibited often enough at the middle management level. More unfortunate is that when it is, it's often buried. Most of the problem stems from characteristics of the traditional management culture. If we're crying about the quality of leadership at the top, it's not surprising that we're not aware of the leadership potential in the middle of our businesses. Yet leadership is happening at both the top and the middle levels of companies, and we'll see even more of it as the 1990s progress. I won't be able to give you many middle management examples of the leadership characteristics I'll be dis-

cussing because business history simply doesn't record them. But you'll have no trouble extrapolating some useful guidelines from my stories of successful business heads who exemplify those characteristics.

The 1990s will be full of opportunity for those of you who want to develop your leadership expertise so that you can head up your own business. Compared to the 1980s, more of you will get the chance to spread your wings and take on businesswide leadership responsibilities. Many of the cultural forces of change have led to the creation of more independent business units. As organizations increasingly sell off units that don't fit their corporate profile, and as they also create stand-alone business units through joint-venture partnerships, more opportunities will arise for managers to lead a business enterprise. Don't discount the possibility that you could apply leadership skills from a position at the top.

Four Rules to Develop Leadership Skills

There's no question that tomorrow's leaders will face a multitude of business challenges. Few of you are in a position to directly set business visions and revise cultures; traditionally, these have been senior management responsibilities. But there will be times when you can take a leadership position on these issues and follow through with indirect actions. The rules I'm about to give you encompass both direct and indirect actions.

Following is a 10–item audit on your company's leadership orientation. A score from 8–10 means that you can spread your wings quickly to develop your leadership style and can expect support from senior managers as you work on leadership issues at your level. A score from 4–7 means that you shouldn't implement these rules too aggressively. Be sure to walk the fine line between being a leader and a cultural threat. A score from 0–3 means be careful! Your company is not yet able to deal with the emerging form of leadership. If you want to take off as a new style of leader, you might want to consider moving to a company that demonstrates an emerging leadership culture.

Audit Your Company for Leadership

Your Company	Traditional Culture	Emerging Culture
——*	1. The vision for the business is seldom discussed and when it is, it is in motherhood terms.	The business vision has tangible meaning at all levels of the organization and serves as a unifying theme.
——	2. People who point out inconsistencies between the actions the business takes and its strategic goals are viewed as negative influences.	People who raise business integrity issues between strategy goals and actions get senior management attention and support.
——	3. It is expected that personal integrity will occasionally be compromised for the good of the business.	People are not put in situations that compromise their personal integrity.
——	4. The company has a textbook corporate management culture.	There are recognized idiosyncrasies in the management culture, but they are positive factors in the company's success.
——	5. Doing things right counts more than doing the right thing.	Doing the right thing is the number-one priority.
——	6. People who challenge the company's sacred cows don't get much support.	If someone is convinced that an unconventional approach is best, it gets a fair hearing.
——	7. Administrative skills get you promoted.	Making a positive difference in the business gets you promoted.
——	8. Managers get upset when their subordinates don't follow standard operating procedures.	Managers encourage subordinates to use their heads first; operating procedures are viewed as guidelines.
——	9. New hires come in with little knowledge of the working environment.	New hires are told war stories so that they know what they are getting into before they join.
——	10. Functional structures are firmly established and determine the basic business direction.	Functional structures are easily and often changed, according to business needs.
—— TOTAL		

*Score 0 point for Traditional Culture; 1 point for Emerging Culture

Rule 1: Make Decisions from an Ownership Perspective

Don't ever confuse leadership with administrative ability. Too often in the past, people rose to the senior management level strictly because of their aptitude for shuffling organizational paperwork and keeping business components glued together. Because we associate leadership responsibilities with senior management positions, it's easy to confuse the two different kinds of skills and to think they overlap. Not only is administrative ability not an indicator of leadership ability, but the two are often in direct conflict.

In the 1980s administrative ability was a key criterion in promotion decisions. Outperforming the budget, delivering mandatory monthly reports on time, maintaining tight staff disciplines—as well as solid justification for every position—and delivering key functional MBO commitments were all signs of a buttoned-up manager who could be trusted to take on bigger responsibilities. These skills are valuable to the company and certainly seem to make a person worthy of promotion. But a manager with only these administrative skills may be badly deficient in leadership credentials.

Let me explain why. A good administrator will always be in total control of his or her area. One way to ensure control and eliminate surprises is to carefully define and narrow your functional responsibilities. Unfortunately, a unit this tightly controlled isn't necessarily effective for the business. Managers who focus on administration don't worry about their unit's contribution to the business unless it affects how well the unit can deliver on its narrowly defined charter. Leaders rip up the charter if it doesn't make business sense, even if the organization has to undergo major change as a result. Leaders worry about doing the right thing with their resources; administrators worry about doing things right.

Government organizations are the classic example of a structure designed to create efficient management administrators. Mission statements and detailed rules about what an agency can and can't do dominate the government culture. Most rules focus on constraining rather than expanding operating freedom. Within this culture, we're breeding some of the best and narrowest administrators in the world. But we're certainly not fostering leaders. Unfortunately, the same can be said of the 1980s corporate environment. If you expect to lead a business, you'll have to give up some of the comfort that goes with being a good administrator. Demands on leaders are much broader than those on administrators.

As a middle manager, you're in the best position to know the details of how your functional area can positively contribute to business decisions. But categorically applied functional inputs can actually weaken good business decisions. Aren't you the one best qualified to inform your company about both the strengths and weaknesses of your unit's functional inputs? But what manager would come clean on weaknesses if doing so puts his or her control of the unit at risk? There aren't many motivations to be this honest in the traditional culture, which doesn't make administrative life easier for managers trying to prove they run tight functional units. In the emerging culture, however, such honesty shows that you can be a leader in delivering the right solutions for the entire organization.

It can be tough to step out of your functional role and broaden your perspective, especially if your business still operates under traditional values. Still, if you carefully select leadership opportunities to act on, you have an enormous chance to set yourself apart from the pack. First, relinquish your faith in the theory that if each function executes its job well, the business will automatically succeed. It may work in the traditional culture, but not in the emerging one. On the other hand, as your business breaks from tradition, don't discount the valuable roles that functions play; it takes tremendous effort to successfully coordinate functions into a unified business. The traditional example of this is the conflict between production and marketing units. When operating plans for the business segments are developed, marketing normally makes specific revenue commitments to justify its budgets. To get the budget allocations, marketing tends to make overly optimistic sales projections. Production budgets are built to support the sales forecasts created by marketing, but good production people wait to see evidence of sales delivery before actually committing extra production resources. When sales come in lower than projected, marketing ends up not achieving its goals while manufacturing overperforms. Through years of experience in integrating these functions, however, people have learned how to properly balance marketing and manufacturing goals. Processes and rules have also been developed to maintain proper business balances and avert conflict between most other functional areas.

These processes and rules are based on well-defined expectations for each function. Whatever the set of expectations in your company, it's important that the functions work together under the general rules. I think most companies would be reluctant to make major overhauls in these rules to accommodate the special needs of just one of their business units. Such conservatism is understandable, but not necessarily smart.

Although changes in functional roles can upset a company's balance, that's no reason to stick to a structure that is no longer working. When change is needed for the good of the business, someone has to initiate it. But if that initiative isn't coming from the top in your company, you don't have to remain passive. There may be indirect actions you can take in your areas of responsibility that will lead to a cohesive business effort among the key functional players.

Don't minimize the benefits of indirect action. Experience has taught me that you can fundamentally change a corporate culture even when you have no explicit responsibility for business culture development. When I joined Campbell Soup in 1978 as vice president for Marketing and Business Development in the Swanson Food Division, my management charter was to lead the division's turnaround and new growth strategy. I had direct responsibility for the marketing function, but none for other functions in the business.

At the time, Swanson was both a success and a failure. It dominated its share of the defined market, frozen TV dinners. But TV dinners were a product of the 1950s, and consumers, their standards raised by the growth of the Stouffer brand, were looking for a higher quality frozen product. While the Swanson brand was clearly successful, most aspects of Swanson production—from creating superior quality to innovative production technology to cost advantages—were all wrong for the modern market. The dilemma was how to get purchasing, manufacturing, and marketing to scrap most of their traditional thinking. Without their endorsement, any changes would be largely cosmetic.

I got a break. Microwave ovens were just coming onto the household scene in the late 1970s, and manufacturers reported a striking purchase pattern. Engineering types bought the appliance for family members, who neither wanted it nor knew what to do with it. So the microwave oven had become known as the great $500 appliance for reheating coffee.

I saw a situation much like the one with color television sets when they were first introduced. Initially, the market was small because so few programs were broadcast in color. But when the networks made the commitment to broadcast in color, the market took off. If a frozen-food manufacturer made the commitment to increase the number of microwavable products on the market, couldn't a real partnership be developed between the oven manufacturers and the food company?

Before the partnership opportunity could be seized, however, it was necessary to change Swanson's internal thinking. Most significantly, we had to get rid of our compartmentalized aluminum trays because metal can't be used in microwave ovens. Thus, the most symbolic, but most negative, component of the 1950s TV dinner had to disappear.

Fortunately, we were able to go ahead not only without attacking any Swanson history but with across-the-board company support. The breakfast market was our first target. Our long-established breakfast line had never sold well because each product took nearly 40 minutes to cook—an unacceptable amount of time for a meal that typically is rushed. By reformulating the product and putting it into microwavable paperboard trays, the cooking time was shortened to three minutes.

Breakfast product sales exploded and led to accelerated commitments to convert the whole Swanson business. Over a three-year period the business culture also changed dramatically. Technological innovation, in both packaging and manufacturing processes, stirred up new life in an organization that had become perhaps too comfortable in its old market niche. One of the new efforts was Swanson's "Le Menu" line of premium dinners, which became the most successful introduction of a major frozen-food brand in 10 years.

Vision and culture were no one's functional responsibility at Swanson, but change occurred anyway because functional managers believed it was important to the overall direction of the business. As we move into the 1990s, business vision and the evolving management culture will only get more important. At the very least, the physical separation of business units will make it necessary for each unit to make and carry out its own priorities. A unit's responsibilities are less likely to stay hidden under the corporate umbrella. In addition, the predicted information technology developments will combine with the effectiveness of more empowered and customer-focused employees to inevitably accelerate the move toward flatter organizations. But it will be increasingly important that senior managers give out clear and consistent messages about the new business vision and culture if these changes are to come about.

Perhaps you recognize that vision and cultural change are critical but feel you don't have the charter to make them a reality. By all means, don't go too far out on a limb, but do look aggressively for other opportunities to better integrate your company's functional areas. The key is convincing functional managers to change their management practices because they believe the changes are right. If they believe you're imposing change on them, you'll get nowhere.

Middle managers have a real opportunity to stake out leadership territory, but they can't afford to ignore the risks. Issues other than functional performance issues often don't get a lot of attention in many of today's corporations. As a result, senior executives tend to evaluate right and wrong business directions from a functional viewpoint rather than with an eye on the overall integration of the management culture. If your company still maintains traditional leadership values, reassess the situation regularly to catch any sign of change. As your company's culture opens up, you can become more aggressive.

How do you maintain your functional performance and still capitalize on opportunities to reshape your company's culture?

It's a delicate balance, but the following suggestions should make it easier to achieve.

First, keep asking yourself if your functional role in the business is playing an important part in the company's success; that is, keep that hypothetical business owner's hat on your head. If your role doesn't seem that important, you need to figure out how to point this out without risking your functional credentials. Remember, you "own" the entire business, not just a single function. So you can raise such an issue if you have great confidence in your predictions about the net gain to the business of changing the size and importance of your functional role.

For instance, I dare the advertising managers among you to hold up your hands and commit to fewer media advertising dollars because the action would benefit your company. Are you a manager who would be willing to do this? If you are, and you know the net gain it would produce for the company, get a commitment to reinvest some of that gain directly into your area so that you can make improvements. Do your homework well, and be sure you understand the perspectives that others will bring to these decisions. In spite of the risk, you could get a big boost in your leadership credentials by taking such an action.

And in spite of the uncertainties, I'm convinced that functional managers can make great contributions to changing organizational visions and cultures. My experience with adapting Swanson frozen TV dinners to the microwavable-food market allowed me to accelerate the advancement of my career at Campbell. I would take this risk again without hesitation. Look for the same opportunities in your own organization, select the most promising ones, and go after them.

Rule 2: Don't Compromise Your Integrity

Whether you're a CEO or a middle manager, as a leader you must enlist the total trust of the people in your organization. It's vital that you develop a clear perspective on your own personal and professional values and principles. You cannot waver on your values and retain any credibility as a trusted leader. Obviously, not all business decisions your company makes will be 100 percent consistent with your personal principles and values. But you're not necessarily compromised by supporting these decisions if you always make it clear to the people in your organization *why* you're supporting them.

For example, "quality" has become the message of choice among flag-waving managers who've gotten enough religion to mouth slogans but not enough conviction to act on them. Such behavior doesn't support the message when the chips are down. Employees quickly spot this kind of inconsistency and the sloganeering starts to have a hollow ring. But leaders acting on their convictions can move businesses to the top of their industries. Such was the case for August A. Busch III.

When August Busch followed in his father's footsteps and became president of Anheuser-Busch in the early 1970s, he was some years away from his fortieth birthday. In addition to the disadvantages of youthfulness, Busch felt pressures on a person taking over a family business. Consider the situation. If he was "given" the job only because of his name, he now had to carry out all the decision-making responsibilities of a top management position, with no qualifications to help him out. If, on the other hand, he did have the qualifications to assume such responsibility at his age, few people were going to give him credit for them, precisely because of his name. To make things even more interesting, Busch was walking into a pressure cooker: the brewery was in trouble. Profits were eroding, and market-share leadership was rapidly shifting to Anheuser-Busch's major competitor, Schlitz.

I consulted for the company during this critical period and saw firsthand some of the strains it created. Anheuser-Busch had always been fanatical about product quality. Traditional and expensive brewing methods, combined with the best ingredients, were at the heart of the company's heritage. The Schlitz strategy was simple. It built high-tech breweries that substantially reduced capital investment requirements and permitted the use of cheaper ingredients. The savings in manufacturing were spent on an aggressive advertising attack on Anheuser-Busch's flagship brand, Budweiser.

The press offered no sympathy. The June, 1973 *Forbes* cover story included an illustration of a glass of beer with no head, carrying the bold headline, "Why Profits Are Flat at Anheuser-Busch." The article graphically detailed the Schlitz strategy and characterized Anheuser-Busch as rigid in its adherence to product quality in the face of the Schlitz onslaught. "Will this dogmatic insistence on product quality standards ruin Anheuser-Busch's success?" *Forbes* asked.

I sat in on a meeting with August Busch and his senior managers when they reviewed the article. From an investor's standpoint, the portrayal of Anheuser-Busch was clearly negative. Busch, however, looked at it from a different point of view. "What would the beer drinker think of Anheuser-Busch and its products," he asked, "if confronted with this information?" Busch bet he knew the answer to that question and acted accordingly.

Within days, reprints of the *Forbes* article began circulating in bars and restaurants. Word of mouth began to build about the company's product quality commitments. A new Anheuser-Busch advertising slogan claimed, "Somebody still cares about quality." Busch won his bet. Schlitz sales peaked shortly thereafter but never recovered. The brand died a painful death.

After this success, Busch never looked back. He became increasingly recognized as one of the most able and qualified executives in the brewing industry and in corporate America. The quality focus is the foundation of the Anheuser-Busch management culture, and August Busch personifies this culture with virtually every action he takes.

Forest Mars built and maintained a culture much like that of the Busch family. Unfortunately, Mars never liked publicity for himself or his enterprise. He was extremely successful, and many corporate executives could have benefited from studying his approach to business.

The Mars Corporation is privately held by the Mars family, allowing it to shut the door on information about the various companies under its corporate umbrella and their operating practices. Forest Mars developed a vast, worldwide, and highly profitable business complex, beginning with a small candy company in England that produced a single product, the Mars Bar. From there, he expanded global businesses in candy (M&Ms, Milky Way, Three Musketeers, and Snickers are the U.S. brands), pet foods (Kal Kan in the United States), and various other foods such as Uncle Ben's rice.

When I consulted for Mars in the early 1970s, shortly after Forest Mars had retired and turned the management of the company over to his children, I saw that his basic principles were well ingrained in all senior managers. Forest Mar's unrelenting focus was on product quality. He established *minimum* percentages of finished product costs that had to be spent on basic ingredients. No, that's not a mistake. Although Mars wanted every area of overhead costs cut, customers were paying for products and he was going to be sure they got what they paid for. This rule thwarted any effort by his managers to expand profits by making small cutbacks in ingredient quality.

My favorite story about Forest Mars illustrates well this focus on delivering quality to the customer. One of his personal beliefs was that the quality of a candy bar is dramatically improved by making it with whole milk rather than condensed or dry milk. You can imagine the quantities of whole milk needed to make all the various Mars candy bars. The roads for miles around a Mars plant were always jammed with tankers delivering fresh milk. The product technicians and industrial engineers knew what a tremendous cost premium this standard created. So once a year they devised experimental formulations of Mars candy bar brands from whole milk and other milk products. Samples of the different formulations underwent extensive consumer taste evaluations to determine whether the differences were noticeable, and each year the tests indicated that few, if any, consumers detected any taste variations. The managers then calculated the savings and developed an impressive presentation for Forest Mars.

Armed with the test results, the managers would take a deep breath, straighten their ties, rehearse their lines, and walk into the president's office. I'm told these meetings almost always followed the same script. First the economics were reviewed. Then the supportive market research was presented. Finally, the sample products were presented for Mars's own taste evaluation. At this point, he would ask the managers which product was made from whole milk. They would try to persuade him to sample the products without knowing, to see whether he could detect any differences. He'd refuse. They would finally identify the product made from whole milk and he would bite into that candy bar only and declare, "It's clearly the best." The meeting would be adjourned.

August Busch and Forest Mars had real advantages in promoting the quality theme because they were not only the chief executives of their companies but they had the long-established credibility of their family names to back them up. As middle managers, you face a greater leadership challenge in getting a quality commitment from your staff, in part because you represent professional management, not family ownership.

Obviously, lacking a family name isn't an insurmountable barrier to promoting quality. Many other professional executives have led the quality revolution for their companies. Some are highly visible, such as Lee Iacocca, who in his Chrysler commercials challenged consumers with, "If you can find a better car, buy it." Most leaders aren't public spokespersons, but almost all share one trait—absolute credibility within their organizations that in their own lives they adhere to the principles they push the organization to adopt.

Your people must see you personally living out your principles as if you were on display in a fishbowl. If they don't, you'll have no credibility and your requests for commitment will seem hollow. Always ask yourself what signals you're really giving the people in your organization about priorities.

Campbell Soup has a real quality culture in its production function that it maintains, in part, with a rule vigorously followed by every level of management: if you walk through the plant, see an employee doing something wrong, and don't stop to correct the mistake, you're basically saying that breaking the rules is okay with you. The Campbell management practice places tremendous, but appropriate, responsibility on the leaders of the organization. If they don't bother to enforce quality standards in the workplace, they are responsible for the damage that results.

Leadership has special burdens, as Lee Iacocca knows from the role he chose to play for Chrysler. The biggest test of the trust he had built in Chrysler advertising was his response to the odometer incident. It was discovered that, after testing cars for a period of time, Chrysler was turning the odometers back to zero and selling the cars as new. Iacocca immediately admitted this corporate deception had occurred and outlined a strategy for dealing with it. By taking the lead in solving the issue, Iacocca gained credibility in the public eye. Had he not stepped forward immediately after the problem surfaced, his media stardom would have crumbled.

Expertise can be another credibility issue. The days when subordinates assumed their manager had more expertise than they did are long gone. The flat organizational structure and the culture of empowerment have made this level of technical expertise practically impossible for managers to acquire and maintain. Think about the newly minted MBAs with fancy salaries but no credibility. Many simply don't have enough detailed knowledge of the business to walk the floor and be able to correct people when they make mistakes. Such a new manager's dilemma is real: should you learn the nuts and bolts of the business, or minimize your time on the front line? I strongly suggest that you admit your inexperience and make people your teachers.

We did just this during our turnaround at Diners Club when we were pushing empowerment concepts. We had one big problem getting the process under way: most of our senior management didn't know what our service representatives did. How could we empower our reps to take on more responsibility if we didn't know what their basic responsibilities were? To bridge the gap, we admitted our deficiencies and created a program called "Walk a Mile in My Shoes." My entire executive committee and I spent several days learning the most basic skills already perfected by our service representatives. The fact that I forgot my computer password the first day of training did more than anything else to bridge the gap: the reps saw that the senior managers really needed their help to learn the ropes. This experience also taught us—and our service reps—that they knew far more about their business than we did, and that they made major contributions to the success of the business through their unique abilities.

To build your leadership credentials, diligently establish your trustworthiness by never compromising your integrity. If everyone in the business both above and below you understands your principles, you'll not only be respected for holding onto them, you will be rewarded with bigger assignments. Some of the most successful leaders in the business world got to the top precisely because of their values.

Rule 3: Establish Team Goals That Are Meaningful to Everyone

Goals and objectives have been a part of the management process for so long that most of us couldn't conceive of running a business without them. Setting performance goals and objectives for managers will certainly continue to be highly valued in the emerging culture. But the goals themselves—both the ones you operate under as a middle manager and the ones you communicate to other people in the organization—will undergo drastic changes.

The changes in goal-setting philosophy are motivated by the recognition that functional units doing their jobs well doesn't ensure that the business will perform successfully. A major leadership challenge in the emerging culture will be looking beyond the specific concerns of a functional area and helping to shape meaningful goals that will make the overall business more successful.

Today managers are often victims of their functional orientation. Finance people see the health of the organization through P&Ls and balance-sheet statements. Production employees are pleased when machines operate at 100 percent capacity with no rejected output. The sales force envisions products moving steadily off the loading dock to customers.

In the past we never had to worry much about unifying functional areas and disciplines. Managers in one functional area could talk their own language and get along quite well among themselves. Integration of the functional areas could be handled by four or five senior executives in executive committee meetings. Even in those simpler times, however, there was always the danger that one function would dominate the business and that success in that area could actually threaten the long-term health of the business. How many times have you heard companies classified as production-driven, marketing-driven, or finance-driven? If a company has this kind of reputation, and deserves it, you can be sure it has vulnerabilities that one or more competitors will eventually exploit.

Today things are changing rapidly and the traditional functional-oriented management goals don't work as well. The business world is becoming far too complicated for managers to indulge individual functions that set their own self-serving goals, expecting a senior management group to sort out any conflicting directions. As organizations flatten and new hybrid functions are created, senior management groups will become increasingly incapable of understanding all the components well enough to be able to properly sort out the functional conflicts. Doing so will more and more become the leadership responsibility of middle managers.

In the emerging culture the traditional goal-setting process for functional units will be reversed. Traditionally, most functions have successfully justified their own growth and expansion by proving the importance of their area to the business at the expense of some other area. "Without our work, massive problems would arise because areas X, Y, and Z would run wild," or, "If it weren't for our work, sales volume would go to zero and everyone else would be out of a job, so we had better get first priority on resources for expansions." The process has been competitive and adversarial and is usually resolved with power and authority decisions coming down from above.

Changing the competitive model won't be easy. The entire U.S. economic system is based on competition. Companies surely prosper when they meet customer needs better and more efficiently than their competitors do. The competitive spirit is so ingrained in our culture that we don't often stop to think about its implications.

We all learn to compete at an early age. Being graded on a curve in school teaches us that our own excellence is relative to that of our peer group. The battle for a spot on the football team or for an acceptance from a first-rate university relays the same message. Your professional advancement is no different. With this background, is it any wonder that your ascent up the managerial ladder is measured against a peer-group standard?

Internal competition was an appropriate way to run a business a decade ago. Now it's a concrete wall. The very structure of the emerging organization makes competition increasingly difficult. How do you measure your success when the company no longer maintains neat hierarchical levels for you to climb? And what does relative progress mean when more people have decision-making power in their independent functions and are linked only by streams of information? It's not as easy anymore as comparing Chrysler and Honda monthly sales reports.

The cultural values of the future generation of U.S. business leaders may already be changing. More and more schools today are deemphasizing winners and losers; instead, for example, kids are encouraged to play games in which no one keeps score. It is certainly possible that this kind of cooperative spirit will change some of the intensely competitive values that have shaped the operating styles of today's companies and their leaders.

One of the surest signs that an organization's goals are dictated by function rather than by team goals is a preponderance of top management authority and directive communication. Senior management must ensure that business operations run smoothly. When they spot functional activities that make little or no sense from their business perspective, they issue new directives to force changes. But functional managers are confused by such moves, since they have been working on goals and objectives that make sense to them. Morale usually plummets when these senior management directives are issued.

A directive style of leadership is clearly incompatible with the emerging cultural values. It's the antithesis of the empowerment principle and is totally incompatible with flat organizational structures and cross-functional networking processes. As managers struggle to adjust to the new cultural philosophy, most of them are trying to move beyond the top-down directive style of leadership.

If a functional unit has goals and objectives that support business directions, there shouldn't be much need for senior management directives to change the course. If goals are truly compatible between management levels, cooperative discussions should be the way to assess whether everyone's priorities are right. When goals aren't compatible, directives are the most efficient way to get the business back on course. But without the understanding that comes from having goals in common, employees find directives from executives to be strikingly similar to those of parents to their children: "Do it because I'm your parent and because I told you so." It's no wonder management by directive destroys morale.

In the traditional culture, everyone in the organization needs to know the who's who of authority levels. Otherwise, no one could be sure whose directive to follow. Obviously, organization charts and hierarchical levels provide the clearest picture. But many companies reinforce positions of authority with some rather obvious clues. The spacious office with an expansive view of the skyline, designer furniture, and plush carpeting you get lost in are all traditional symbols that not so subtly tell employees which managers carry the most clout. These symbols have worked in the traditional environment, but they inhibit efforts to change to the emerging culture.

When John Reed took over as CEO of Citicorp, he had to make leadership changes. One of Reed's most important objectives was to make Citicorp a global financial powerhouse. He sought to unleash the bank's collective resources and build the Citicorp presence in every corner of the world. He knew that to achieve his goal, he had to have much closer cooperation between the various units of the corporation in each country and global markets. Otherwise, he would not be taking full advantage of Citicorp resources to achieve his global vision. Traditionally, the bank had focused on customer functions, such as consumer banking, corporate banking, and institutional banking. Reed hoped that implementing a teamwork approach in these traditional functions at the top of Citicorp would signal to units at the country level that teamwork was going to be Citicorp's successful new strategy.

One of Reed's leadership strategies for communicating the change to the organization was to change the traditional symbols of authority and power in the bank. He redesigned the executive office environment to signal the new emphasis on teamwork. Reed made all the executive offices the same size, including his own. All the functional executives had adjacent offices with open glass fronts to encourage walk-in communication. A Japanese rock garden was created in a common area to facilitate informal conversations.

No one missed Reed's clue. He knew he could not change

overnight a corporate culture with traditional stand-alone units around the world into one with units that worked together in each global market. But the changes he made at corporate headquarters made it clear that he expected a cultural change to eventually be made. In fact, his own changes in the executive offices accelerated the overall process of change at Citicorp.

Whether or not you get a direct signal from your top management, I don't think you should wait for such a signal before changing your own goal-setting process. Whatever your specific functional responsibilities, you can work to establish goals that link up to those of the total organization and simultaneously use them to build team-oriented goals across and down your own organizational units. I have no doubt that you will have a chance to be a leader in setting team goals. It's up to you to spot the opportunities when they come and then figure out how to capitalize on them.

I talked with a manager from an energy resource company who faced the challenge of fusing different functions into a cohesive team to launch a new business opportunity. "I was responsible for building $1 billion worth of power plants for my corporation. I found that the various fragments of the organization all thought they had the final say in how the plan ought to be put together. Every group believed its part was absolutely critical to the mission's success and the hell with everyone else. But no one had a real grasp of how the various cells interrelated with one another, and worse, no one had a handle on what we were trying to do, where we were going, or why.

"I decided to hold a three-day retreat for people involved from within my organization as well as outside the company—engineers, construction personnel, auditors, environmentalists—everyone who played a role in the project. We actually role-played: for instance, what would happen if the test engineers didn't do their job or the mechanical engineers didn't do theirs—how it would set back the entire project. I was trying to build a team, to emphasize that if we all worked together, we could accomplish our goal faster and more easily, for less money. They'd never been through anything like it before.

"But we came out of the retreat as a unified group, understanding how our work interfaced with others. And in fact, we continued to hold meetings."

A manager for a large utility company didn't fare as well. With customers who were billed more than $10 million a year, no unit of the business wanted to relinquish control of its expense dollars to another unit to establish a much-needed customer service program. In other words, "I'll keep it all in-house, and you can offer your own service to the customer. Get your expense money directly from the customer with increased rates tied to your offering, since you won't get the dollars from me." In this kind of situation, the customer always loses because no unit will fund another to consolidate the service offering—a common theme, unfortunately, when a culture is operated from a functional rather than a business perspective.

Although linking the goals for your area to your company's business goals is vital to the development of your leadership skills, don't get hung up if you initially have trouble tying your activities directly to the overall business. The important thing is that you start formulating goals that expand beyond your narrow functional responsibilities. Once you've made this stretch in your goal-setting philosophy, you can stretch even further at the appropriate time.

Your best opportunity to shine might not actually be establishing the goal but creatively achieving it. To get people's attention, goals must be meaningful and relevant to all employees. Otherwise, they will not bind the group together, and you'll still have individual players working on personal goals, not team players working on team goals. So be creative, but keep one important warning in mind: financial formulations of goals usually affect only a small number of your employees. The goals that have the best impact on an organization normally are not grounded in financial numbers.

I saw what a worthwhile team goal could do for a business while I was at Campbell Soup. I had acquired the company Juice Bowl in 1981 as part of a diversification strategy for our juice business. The quick and successful integration of Juice Bowl into our Beverage Business Unit was critical to broadening our beverage range, and I was worried about how to do it.

Juice Bowl was a $50 million family-held business in Lakeland, Florida. I bought the company because it offered a beautiful fit to our own strategy. Jack Grady, the company's president and owner, brought his key management team to the New Jersey

Campbell headquarters for the official signing of the sale. The morning after, we traveled to Napoleon, Ohio, the site of our major midwestern juice-processing plant. The size of the Napoleon plant and the sophistication of our operations somewhat intimidated the Juice Bowl team. Yet I had seen the can-do attitude of these people and was certain that their creativity and the speed with which they implemented innovation would help them to play a key role in the Campbell system.

One of the first items on our agenda was planning the production of Juice Bowl products at our Napoleon plant and the production of our V-8 and tomato juice at their Lakeland plant. The plan was to be ready for the exchange by April 1982, six months after the purchase. While discussing the logistics of the production swap, I discovered that each December, Juice Bowl held a Founders Day dinner for everyone with five years or more seniority. Why not try to get V-8 produced at Lakeland in time for the dinner? The Juice Bowl team jumped at the chance to prove its skills.

We made it, but barely. At 4:00 P.M. on the day of the dinner, we produced our first batch of V-8 out of Lakeland and served it at the dinner. Nothing could have gotten us off to a better start than this visible symbol of our successful integration—accomplished four months earlier than the Campbell people had said it could be done. As I spoke at the Founders Day dinner, I could see pride written all over every face. I knew then that we had a success on our hands.

A director for a large computer company managed to overcome traditional thinking when he proposed something unheard of at his company: acquire a business. "The case was pretty clear for buying the business, but ours isn't a company that likes acquisitions. So before trying to convince senior management, we held formal and informal reviews with the groups that would be most affected by the new business. We worked to answer their objections and anticipate problems that could be created. We even held preliminary conversations with a member of senior management whose endorsement would carry a lot of weight.

"We did encounter initial resistance from the financial end of the business because they believed there simply couldn't be that high a return on an acquisition. So we got the finance group to review the books with us—that way they weren't just listening to our story; they were participating in it. We followed the same procedure with other organizations that resisted the idea.

"What could have been a single group developing some hare-brained idea, became a team that took a partnered proposition to the executive office. For someone trying to get something done quickly, this might sound like the long way around. But the reality is that had we not followed this procedure, it would have taken three to four times as long—if it could have been done at all. As it turned out, we acquired the business, and profits have thus far supported our suspicions that the business would add a great deal of value to the entire corporation."

You might be surprised at the number of opportunities there are to set your own goals in such a way as to motivate the whole organization. With a careful plan that includes enlisting the support of all available resources, you can gain the support of even the most traditional company. But opportunities don't arise only when you're producing the annual operating plan, so keep your eyes and ears open for them.

Rule 4: Develop Your Own Leadership Style and Find a Place to Flourish

Sometimes tension arises between the values and culture of one business unit and the traditional culture of the parent corporation. You can't ignore such tension if both organizations are to succeed in the marketplace.

Perhaps the most famous cultural inconsistency occurred when Ross Perot sold his EDS business to General Motors and attempted to integrate its culture with that of GM. Perot had built a very special culture at EDS. He recruited staff who fit into the culture, and he made no apologies about the type of environment he wanted to create. Perhaps the only mistake he made in shaping the culture was in not assessing how fundamentally different it was from GM's and how resistant GM would be to accepting the EDS culture.

I watched this same tension come to a head between Campbell

Soup and one of its businesses, Godiva Chocolate. Godiva was an anomaly in the Campbell organization. Although it used food manufacturing technologies that Campbell understood well, its product was marketed as an upscale, luxury item more suited to the fashion industry than the food industry. Godiva's entire marketing process and its business economics were different from the rest of Campbell's business. For instance, the product was sold at places like Bloomingdale's, not Kroger's or Wal-Mart. Far from having cents-off coupons as part of its marketing plan, Godiva hired fashion models to attract shoppers to its counter displays.

The person then heading Godiva had an appropriate background for the business, and Godiva had taken off under his leadership. But his management style and approach to product marketing greatly concerned the corporate staff at Campbell. They didn't feel the business could stay successful when it operated so differently from the way they were used to.

The new Godiva president didn't understand the Campbell culture any more than they understood his. Because he was setting sales records, the corporate staff weren't in a position to challenge his methods. The Godiva president took great delight in teasing and frustrating the Campbell traditionalists; at one point a rumor swept the corporate offices that Godiva had ordered a chocolate-colored Lear jet for making calls on key customers. The rumor was totally unfounded, but the Godiva management team loved playing it up.

When the Godiva president decided to leave the company to pursue a bigger opportunity, Campbell faced a cultural dilemma. No one within Godiva was experienced enough to take on the presidency, but the Campbell managers didn't fit the company's culture. Campbell finally decided to fill the position with a Campbell manager. The business's record growth momentum quickly dissipated, along with the cultural philosophy that had created it.

One challenge in the 1990s will be to minimize the number of starts and stops the emerging culture experiences as it tries to settle in and maintain an even keel. The best way to do this is to nurture talent from within each business unit, giving greater responsibility to those managers who are philosophically tuned into the total culture created by the leader. That will mean corporations who own many independent business units need to get comfortable with widely varying cultural styles under the same roof. As a result of this increased cultural diversity, you'll need to spend more time getting comfortable defining the right one for you.

During my consulting years, I worked with several organizations with management cultures that worked for them but that could never have worked as part of a traditional conventional corporation. One such culture supported a business complex started by Cloyce Box.

A prototypical Texas entrepreneur, Cloyce Box was a ruggedly handsome football player from West Texas State who played for the Detroit Lions during the 1950s. After his football days were over, his interests turned toward business. Through a series of rapid job moves, Box found himself president and CEO of OKC, a New York Stock Exchange conglomerate. Beginning with a core cement business, he added businesses in oil refining and exploration and also picked up a dredging company along the way.

When I met Cloyce Box in 1978 at his home (used as the South Fork Ranch in the television series "Dallas"), we discussed a consulting project to "help us make smarter decisions about how we grow the company." The project was designed to help Box think through the strengths and weaknesses of existing business bases in OKC and to sharpen the company's perspective on where it ought to go. But even designer fashions don't comfortably fit all people, and it became clear that traditional approaches to growth decisions did not fit Cloyce Box.

The conflict between Box's entrepreneurial style and a disciplined strategic plan was vividly illustrated during one of our lunch meetings. An option under consideration was to get out of the oil business altogether. Box and I discussed the implications of OKC becoming almost totally dependent on the cement business for its earnings. Since cement was a boom-or-bust venture, I asked if OKC was prepared for the earnings volatility that would result. Box responded that he was convinced the businesses would not be affected by such cycles. "Why?" I asked. "Because we sell a premium product and can get our prices regardless of market conditions." I scratched my head in bewilderment and frustration when he couldn't give me one reason why his cement was so different from other companies.' I tried another tactic.

I told him that if he was correct, his salespeople should be able to get premium prices for OKC cement. "We could if we wanted to." So I suggested we test this premise by having his salespeople charge premium prices to prove it could be done. "Great idea," he said. "We'll do it." I thought I had Box where I wanted him. "Now suppose," I said, "that it turns out your people are unable to sell the cement at premium prices?" Box instantly responded, "I'd fire them." At that point I realized that OKC operations would continue to reflect Cloyce Box's entrepreneurial style, and that textbook strategic analysis would play little part in the company's decision-making process. I also had to admit it was difficult to argue with the track record he'd established.

If you're going to play an effective leadership role in your organization from a middle management position, be absolutely certain you can support the values of the business culture for your people. Be sure you're comfortable with your organization's overall structure, not just with individual values. For example, Citicorp supports both its business units and its managers according to the merits of their accomplishments. This core value fosters a stronger entrepreneurial focus than most other corporations are able to maintain. This core value is reflected in Citicorp's performance rating system, which ranks all employees in the company's population. The system ensures that compensation will accrue to those who accomplish the most because of an outstanding level of performance; it also fosters competition because each employee's performance is judged relative to that of all other employees. Even within Citicorp, the competitive rating process is somewhat controversial. But it's consistent with a corporate culture that encourages individual accomplishments. Every corporation will have individual cultural elements that invite controversy. Make sure you don't get so focused on those elements that you compromise your support for the overall system.

Shaping Leadership Opportunities

As you prepare for the 1990s, recognize that tomorrow's leaders will be those people who build corporate cultures based on clear visions for their organizations. Develop a career that reflects your basic convictions about management. People need to know where you stand and that your values and principles are sound. Build your managerial integrity; it will become increasingly valuable as more companies seek out those with leadership skills appropriate to the emerging culture. Whether you're the head of a business or a middle manager, your leadership abilities depend on your integrity never being questioned or compromised.

Being able to capitalize on leadership opportunities boils down to your willingness to take the risks and grab them when they arise. Playing it safe won't cut it. If opportunity so much as scratches at your door, open that door and welcome the chance to make a bold, calculated move. Leadership isn't reserved for a select few at the top, and you'll have your chance to prove that.

6

The Fourth Key Experience: Building Experiences with Taking Risks

The idea of taking business risks causes some people to suffer a panic attack, while others look forward to the challenge. But all of today's managers are faced with competitive forces that demand bold actions. The days of the passive manager are long gone, if only because the relative dearth of available management positions mandates that all managers take initiatives that contribute to the overall business. Managers must first decide which risks are important enough to take, and then actively manage them.

Risk Avoidance in the Traditional Culture

Do you know managers in your company who year after year seem to always be on the winning side of key decisions? With a remarkable sense of timing, they commit to a position on an issue just before final decisions are made. When issues first arise, they straddle the fence, but they ultimately declare their position, and in highly visible ways. After making their declaration, they work like hell to move to the head of the parade so as to own as much of the glory as possible. Such individuals are the most skilled risk managers in the traditional management culture. They're not innovative, but you'll never find them out on a limb on a losing issue either.

There's another type of traditional manager who exploits risk management for personal gain. You probably know managers who fit this mold. They get the rules down pat on how decisions will be evaluated and then dogmatically apply those rules because "that's the way the senior guys view the world." These managers often shut down good ideas because they don't conform to the predefined measurement of success.

These are the management styles of those who manage risk by avoiding it. In the traditional culture, many managers built their careers by steering clear of risk. However successful this career strategy may have been in the past, I believe risk management skills in the emerging culture will require much more from managers than successfully avoiding risk. Put yesterday's risk management role models on the sidelines. There's a new ball game on the field.

Risk management has always been a part of the management process, whether organizations deal with it consciously or unconsciously. Every time a management team faces uncertainty about a decision they're taking (and what decision doesn't involve some measure of uncertainty?), it must weigh the possible ways things could go wrong against the gains to be made if everything turns out all right. Economists have a theory about such risk decisions: actions that involve greater uncertainty ought to yield a larger return. Thus, if a management group is going to make a high-risk gamble, it had better guarantee that the gamble will pay off sizable returns. If that guarantee can't be made, walk away from the risk. But if taking the risk truly has home-run possibilities, the organization should be willing to believe the decision to take it is worthwhile, whether it succeeds or fails.

Okay, that's the theory. And it does work reasonably well in some well-defined areas, such as the relationship between the creditworthiness of a company and what it pays to borrow money. But even this application works far from perfectly. If organizations handling credit ratings use a system that doesn't fit a particular company's real picture of its risk, the company, not the credit rating network, is likely to adapt. In other words, the company will produce a picture of its financial health that fits what the credit raters are looking for.

In the 1980s corporate environment, most companies didn't do a good job of risk management. Senior executives often didn't have a complete picture of the risks involved in particular decisions. The communication links down and across the organization weren't strong enough to give them all the facts. So a middle manager would be handed a project for which expectations and results were very different because of the distorted perspectives on it. If the middle manager and the senior executive weren't on the same wavelength, the manager was often penalized for taking actions that might have been right for the business but were wrong from his boss's point of view.

One of the factors contributing to poor risk management processes in the 1980s was the move by corporations to delineate employees' responsibilities more specifically and measure their performances more quantitatively. Unfortunately, not all business risks are measurable or fall into neat areas of management responsibility. And when risks can't be defined or measured categorically, managers have an inevitable and classical dilemma on their hands: should they play by the narrow rules and manage risk as their boss expects them to, or should they try to do what's right for the business?

Risk Management in the Emerging Culture

I believe the emerging culture will facilitate better risk management processes. We're empowering people to take action when the first signals appear that something is in need of fixing, and encouraging them to stop burying risks in the hope that they will go away. We're also investing in new and better business options well before deterioration in the business numbers forces us to make changes. Business partnerships are a good example of the change in thinking—they are increasingly undertaken up front in a project to reduce risk through shared expertise.

We also have a much more enlightened view of how to tie performance objectives to bonuses. A decade ago, if managers failed to achieve the numbers spelled out in their MBOs by the end of the year, they missed bonus payments. Period. No discussion. Many of them had made outstanding contributions to the business, but they fell victim, at least financially, to the system because it had so little flexibility in assigning and revising performance targets.

Changing MBOs and consequently revising the relation between risk and reward for managers could be the most important change happening in risk management processes. We will now change the performance targets if the logic is right. Managers won't be hung out to dry because they originally committed to MBO numbers that are no longer appropriate.

Admittedly, there will always be gray areas. Today's senior managers should recognize that it's essential to explicitly address the risk involved in all decisions. If it's not addressed, rewards will follow only the managers who deliver successful results. Who would be crazy enough to sign up to manage a project that has a one-in-ten chance of doubling the company's size, but failure to deliver the success would create a professional black mark? If absolute success is the only criterion by which managers are judged, organizations will cling to the most conservative, short-term behaviors imaginable.

We must not forget that the struggle to unleash corporate America's talent for bold innovation depends on senior managers' ability to create environments in which high-risk, high-return options are treated appropriately. Middle managers haven't jumped at the chance to become involved in these ventures in traditional cultures because the career risks are too great. As this changes, new opportunities will open up for middle managers.

Senior executives in most companies are working to strengthen both the quality of decisions and individual reward systems. But it's a daunting task. One day they're directing their people to do what's right for the company's long-term growth; the next day they're confronted by a pack of Wall Street analysts beating the hell out of them with quarterly earnings reports and industry performance ratios that increasingly make no sense in today's business culture.

One irony of this dilemma is perhaps best illustrated by the phenomenon known as the "corporate writeoff." It's well documented that the stock of most companies goes up when senior executives announce a major writeoff of a "bad investment." Despite the earnings tumble that results, management is perceived to be showing its commitment to abandoning strategies that don't work. You have to wonder why Wall Street is excited about such action when the company is also walking away from any possibility of future revenues from the written-off projects. No sensible manager would touch those projects under any conditions. But does it make sense to abandon all high-risk ventures so completely when they get off track? And should Wall Street applaud such action as often as it does?

Forces for Better Risk Management Processes

Business partnerships, especially international ones, will be an important factor in creating new commitments to managing risk in the emerging corporate environment. Global partnerships are seen as the essential foundation for long-range strategies, even for the largest and most diverse companies in the world. Companies must be willing to assume the inherent risks of global partnerships and joint ventures because the potential returns are equally large. If a company's culture doesn't support such risk-taking, its survival could be the biggest risk it must manage.

Bold and innovative moves, such as forging partnerships, won't succeed if managers sit on the sidelines, passively waiting for just the right moment to leap onto what appears to be the winning bandwagon. The global challenges of the 1990s are scary for companies stuck in the 1980s culture and staffed with terrified, permanent fence sitters. And they are hardly encouraged by the fact that many people who opted to play it safe in the 1980s today sit in senior management positions. They were rewarded for running the business smoothly, for not taking chances. These executives and their cultural habits might be the reason most new product efforts by American companies are less than innovative, poor in return, and getting worse by the year.

Look at your own company: how many of your senior managers got there by taking a big gamble and coming out a winner? More important, how many took a big gamble on an idea that failed miserably? If your company has a typical traditional culture, most of its executives did neither. Chances are they're smart, articulate, hard-nosed professionals who, when handed a business with good growth momentum, have taken the "right," safe actions to extend that momentum for a few more years. And when they've been handed a business in trouble, more often than not they have cut losses and withdrawn funds. They have been caretakers of the short—term bottom line.

This management style is already changing and will continue to do so simply because this change is absolutely crucial to surviving in the 1990s. The successful managers who avoided risks during the 1980s won't be the right role models for the future. You'll do yourself a favor by not trying to emulate them.

Five Rules to Develop Risk Management Skills

I'm convinced that acquiring risk management skills will strengthen the résumé of any middle manager seeking advancement opportunity over the next 10 years. Place a big priority on honing such talents. Remember, it's easy to get trapped into following strategies that worked in the past. But the rules change because of forces like the globalization of business.

Get a lead on your company's risk orientation by using the following 10-item audit. As with the company audits for the other three key experiences, your company's score on risk issues will help you balance your strategy for capitalizing on the rules I provide. If your company scores 8–10, it will understand and support you in taking bold steps to apply the rules of risk management. At a score of 4–7, you will find your company's support diminishing if you decide to take on high risk/high return projects; at 0–3, your support is practically nonexistent.

Audit Your Company for Risk Taking

Your Company	Traditional Culture	Emerging Culture
____*	1. Risk-taking is viewed as something to avoid.	Risk-taking is viewed as an opportunity as long as the risks involve potential returns.
____	2. Programs that fail are swept under the rug.	Program disappointments (*failure* isn't considered an appropriate word) are viewed as an opportunity to learn.
____	3. Managing something that fails is a major black mark on a manager's career advancement.	How a manager handles a project is more important to his or her career than the outcome.
____	4. The best executives in the company run the big established businesses.	The best executives run the businesses that present the greatest challenges and opportunities.
____	5. The company's management group is professional, mobile, and unlikely to have made long-term commitments to the company.	The management group has significant stock ownership in the company and a long-term commitment to it.
____	6. People change job assignments often within the company.	People stay in a job over extended periods, driven by the commitment to see key projects through from beginning to end.
____	7. Incentive pay is based on results delivered in the previous year.	Incentive pay is based on contributions to long-term business success.
____	8. People stick to the rules on how things are done.	People are encouraged to try new and sometimes crazy things as long as they don't "blow the place up."
____	9. Quantitative analysis and return-on-investment models drive most decisions.	Both qualitative and quantitative factors are considered in management decisions.

*Score 0 point for Traditional Culture; 1 point for Emerging Culture

Traditional Culture	Emerging Culture	Your Company
10. Projects are explicitly classified as successes or failures, usually based on meeting minimal financial returns.	Projects aren't classified as successes or failures because too many factors affect the final judgment.	——
		——
		TOTAL

I believe the stakes involved in getting the balance right between your development and that of your company are higher in the risk area than for any of the other three key experiences. The higher risk-return ratio gives you an added reason to sharpen your skills. They could be the difference between losing your job if you make a foolish commitment and moving to the executive suite if you get it right.

If your company condemns people who are responsible for areas that perform below expectations, don't go after high-profile, high-risk jobs. If you're in one of those areas right now, work your way out of it as quickly as possible. It's simply not worth it to take this kind of uncontrolled risk and then to be judged so narrowly. But if your company promotes risk-taking as an important element of career advancement, you'll want to get busy assessing which risk opportunities are worthwhile and how to pursue them.

Rule 1: Measure Meaningful Risks against the Returns

As a middle manager, you must ask the right questions about any risky project or venture you're thinking about joining within your company. Get key issues resolved up front with senior managers through both formal and informal processes. If you don't, the company will invariably veer toward running the venture too safely and making investments in it that will be too conservative.

Whether you're in on the recommending, approving, or executing end of such projects, you can play an important role by ensuring that the ground rules are clearly established before the first dollar is spent. There are three questions to ask:

- How big could the project be if it's successful?
- How much are we willing to spend to make it a reality?
- What are the odds for success?

Each answer is a judgment call. Although certain analytic processes can help, answering these questions usually involves subjective, gut-level judgments.

When the ground rules have been defined, the project team can garner a win for itself in at least three ways besides hitting a home run:

- It can increase the odds for project success.
- It can determine that the project doesn't make sense, saving the company a substantial amount of money in coming to this conclusion.
- It can determine that the potential benefits of a success are even greater than first anticipated.

Any of these three alternative ways for a project team to succeed can be meaningful to the organization. But if the risk parameters are not defined from the start, it's possible that the only success that will count in the eyes of senior management is ultimate venture success. Far fewer qualified managers will risk a career blemish to get involved in such an effort.

In my professional experience, managing risk isn't well understood or executed by many companies. I joined Citicorp partly because I felt the company had adopted an enlightened outlook on managing risk, an outlook that is well reflected in its public image as having an aggressive, risk-taking, entrepreneurialistic management.

In doing my homework on the pluses and minuses of taking on the Diners Club challenges, Citicorp's well-developed risk management process was a key factor. Diners Club was a high-risk assignment, and I wanted to be sure I was working for a company that understood the issues. My actual management experiences at Diners Club confirmed the accuracy of my perception of its parent company. A book written by former Citicorp chairman Walter Wriston shortly after he turned the chairmanship over to John Reed provides great insight into the values that drive Citi-

corp. The following quotes from *Risk and Other Four-Letter Words* (1986) reflect Wriston's philosophy of risk management:

> The essential difference between the bureaucrat and the entrepreneur is the willingness to take risks. But without the risk-takers, the bureaucrats will ultimately have nothing to administer or regulate.

> Risk is a necessary part of life and one that belongs on our list of natural rights.

> Uncertainty is the opportunity to make the world a better place.

Wriston's message is clear: risk is something you can't avoid; in fact, you should seek it out. Too many managers treat risk as if it's an incurable disease: they try to manage risks away rather than treating them as opportunities to be exploited.

The first risk is identifying which risks to tackle. Just keep in mind that risk is nothing more than that measure of uncertainty about the outcome of actions taken. The key is not to minimize uncertainty but to ensure that where it's greatest, the opportunities are likewise greatest.

A manager with a large newspaper organization told me how his company almost pulled away from an excellent opportunity simply because of the fear surrounding a risky business venture. "We uncovered an exciting telecommunications challenge and began to launch the product. As we got further into the project, we discovered that the internal evaluation of the new product differed greatly from the business plan going in. But our functionally driven company, with its traditional controls, wasn't comfortable starting up and evaluating a new product although we were attempting to play an innovative role in the industry.

"The second week following the product's launch, my boss asked me to seriously consider shutting down the project—even though the financial break-even point was two years out. The underlying reason? Simply that anything truly innovative is difficult for a culture such as ours. We were looking at real fear of lost credibility on the part of senior management in a high-risk venture. My boss even made it quite clear that he was concerned about what the project's failure could mean for his career.

"The product answered industry needs for long-term success. It was an example of what we should be doing. That's the paradox. We have a consensus in the industry that products like this are required for long-term growth, but our internal culture prohibits taking the risk. So my company really is saying, maintain a business-as-usual outlook and hope for the best rather than plan for the future."

If you are confident that the risk-return ratio is properly balanced, no one should criticize investments in such projects. Just keep asking, "Is the return potential worth the uncertainty I have assumed and am living with?" And always try to discuss key expectations about the venture before any major investments and commitments are made. It doesn't matter what facet of the venture you're responsible for; consensus on the risk involved makes everyone's job go better.

Be sure your boss is aware of all the risks associated with the venture, even if your decision about it was to take no action—often the riskiest action you can take. People need to understand the facts behind the options. Too often, managers groomed in the 1980s have been afraid to inform their superiors about emerging environmental conditions.

Review these key risk issues at every project meeting. If you're involved in a later stage of the venture—say, as a member of the execution team—try to get the project team to retrace the logic of the decision and expectations about it if these aren't clear. Doing so could be tough, but be as persistent as possible. Logic is always on your side, and very difficult to fight.

If you can't win a particular battle, protect yourself from being unfairly scapegoated. Don't get caught holding the bag on a losing effort. Instead, begin right away preparing yourself for the inevitable next round of risk decisions. Over time you'll win.

Rule 2: Break the Mold of Conventional Thinking to Stimulate Innovation, Especially for High-Risk, High-Return Ventures

If you've succeeded in getting senior management endorsement of a high-risk, high-return project, you now have a supreme opportunity. You can stimulate the creativity of the execution team in ways its members might never have experienced. Maybe you can awaken energies in the team that will lead to the breakthrough that never happened under tight-leashed management. When managers strive to ensure that something measurably positive comes out of every project investment, the stimulated thinking that results in breakthroughs is often sacrificed.

Sometimes the best way to get a breakthrough is to make this the real objective. Leaders can accomplish this by setting standards for minimally acceptable performance that simply can't be met in the conventional ways. The most important part of setting such standards is convincing the organization that without a breakthrough the business is totally stalemated. When employees believe this is the case, creative energies on new solutions begin to flow.

Campbell employees responded precisely this way when we were searching for a healthy juice alternative to Hi-C and Hawaiian Punch. These products are essentially sugar-water formulations, with 10 percent juice thrown in to placate nutritional-conscious parents. We knew kids liked the taste of the products even if most parents didn't buy the nutrition story. We set three goals for a new beverage line. First, we wanted 100 percent juice products with no added sugar. Second, we wanted kids to prefer the taste of our beverages. Finally, we wanted the selling price to be no more than 15 percent greater than the price of Hi-C and Hawaiian Punch.

The product development group screamed in protest. How could these three conditions be met simultaneously? The greatest obstacle was developing a costly pure juice product while meeting the price condition. "Impossible!" the group declared. But after unsuccessfully testing senior management resolve on these conditions for several months, creative thinking took off.

The breakthrough came while a technician was studying new canned-fruit products packed in natural juice instead of sugar-water solutions. The Hawaiian pineapple processors had perfected a juice by-product of the pineapple-slicing process. By capturing and squeezing the last juice from the pineapple shells after cutting the fruit, processors were able to filter and clarify the juice to create a natural juice product with virtually no taste. It was essentially a juice alternative to sugar water, recaptured from processing by-products that would normally have been thrown out. The new basic ingredient in canned-fruit products was practically cost-free and could be sold to fruit packers for a price slightly higher than that of standard sugar solutions.

We obtained a government ruling to ensure that the by-product remained classified as a natural juice, thus achieving the breakthrough we were looking for. Had we not been so insistent on the conditions our new product had to meet, I'm certain product technicians wouldn't have identified the fruit-processing by-product as our low-cost solution.

It's easy to be satisfied with processes and actions that lead to slight improvements. After all, by multiplying "slight" by the resources of the whole organization, you can create some impressive total progress. Thinking that breaks the mold is rare, often because management hasn't seriously challenged the organization to do it. When you can afford the risk of a total failure, you have the perfect opportunity to establish and adhere to performance standards that force breakthrough thinking.

Rule 3: Avoid Criticizing a High-Risk, High-Return Proposition That Fails

How an organization handles the failure of a high-risk venture will be critical to its overall success in the emerging culture. Prepare a positive way for anyone involved in such efforts to reenter the business. If possible, define the reentry strategy at the project's start.

Try to ensure that corporate shame doesn't fall on a failed high-risk undertaking. This occurs when senior managers refuse to discuss or learn from such a venture. They are embarrassed by the failure, tired of getting the bad news reports, and eager to get out of the situation as painlessly as possible. When senior managers reach this mind-set, it's too late to revive their support. But the worst you can do is treat the project like another skeleton to be entombed in the corporate closet. Instead, try to create an atmosphere in which the occasional failure is accepted; without it, your company will never take the big risks that can have such great rewards.

I encountered a classic case of unshakeable traditional thinking in 1978 when I consulted for Weyerhauser, the forest products company. The company was committed to launching new business ventures that could create significant profit growth. The management group involved was given marching orders to "swing for the fences." Weyerhauser wasn't interested in small ideas that would only nibble at the company's financial position.

A new material that created great excitement at Weyerhauser was called Product 714. It was a composite material made primarily of wood fiber with plastic resin. The Weyerhauser business development group quickly identified the replacement of soft-drink metal cans as a major target application for Product 714. The executive group was enthusiastic; if the product could be perfected, the potential volume was enormous. Furthermore, with the public's growing environmental concerns, Weyerhauser felt it had a significant marketing advantage in using a renewable resource, trees, as the primary material. What the company didn't appreciate, however, were the difficult technological issues it would face.

The early enthusiasm for the product may have done a disservice to the project team responsible for it. Senior management was aware of project deadlines but was committed to making available whatever financial resources were needed to meet them. Unfortunately, as the months, then the years, went by, the financial drain accelerated and progress ground to a halt. Attitudes about Product 714 began to shift on executive row.

The pressure on the project team to produce was unrelenting. Late in the venture, the team took a step back and asked if the material was equally or better suited for other applications besides beverage containers. The answer was "probably yes." Product 714 had promise as a lightweight replacement for metal parts in the automotive industry, as well as for making lightweight but sturdy luggage. It even had potential as a component of low-cost housing in Third World countries. But the time for Product 714 had come and gone.

The material was single-mindedly viewed by senior management as part of a beverage container product, and that was that. When the last executive advocate retracted his support, the plug was pulled—and pulled completely. After that decision, Weyerhauser had an opportunity to license the technology and manu-facturing for Product 714 to another company. But it was clear that Weyerhauser had lost all appetite for the product; the answer was no. Whatever the financial gains from such an agreement, Weyerhauser couldn't face the possibility of another company making a success of a product over which it had failed so badly.

Throughout the 1980s businesses adopted this type of strategy and redoubled their efforts to ensure the success of a proven business formula. This made sense at a time when managers worried more about being blamed for failure than about leading their company to make the right decision at the right time. Even with new competitive challenges, it's easy to see why risk of failure would prompt a manager to stick with the proven formula.

Obviously, the 1980s culture didn't drive all managers to fear being blamed for failure. Examples of such decisions stand out because they are relatively rare. A tragic example involved the largest, single-day massacre of its kind in U.S. history. In San Ysidro, California, a small and religious community outside San Diego, McDonald's was a favorite gathering spot for families and friends. It was there, on the otherwise uneventful afternoon of July 18, 1984, that a gunman opened fire, killing 21 people.

Immediately, McDonald's president, Mike Quinlan (now chairman), and other company executives boarded a plane for San Diego. Throughout the solemn days that followed, the company executives were in San Ysidro to carry out the company's decision to disclose all details about the incident to the public. Open communication was imperative if McDonald's was to do the right thing for the victims and their families and survivors. Although McDonald's was certainly not responsible for the shooting, management decided to take full responsibility for the impact the tragedy would have on the close-knit community.

The empty restaurant began to exude a shrinelike quality to the community and its survivors. Consulting with community and religious leaders, McDonald's decided to demolish the building and donate the land for community use in memory of those slain. In handling the incident, P&L statements were the furthest thing from Quinlan's mind, and sizable financial assistance was and is still being provided to several people affected by it. Although McDonald's could have been an easy target for sensationalist headlines, the public instead perceived the company as a victim of circumstance, owing to Quinlan's efforts to establish honest, frank communication and to provide comfort and assistance to the San Ysidro community.

Johnson & Johnson took visible risks with its Tylenol business on several occasions. The best known is the company's response during the first critical days after cyanide was discovered in its Extra Strength Tylenol capsules. Seven people died.

Having almost no knowledge of the problem's source or magnitude, Johnson & Johnson abandoned all thoughts of financial issues in its decisions and moved aggressively to do the right thing to protect the public. Jim Burke, Johnson & Johnson's chairman, took on the role of explaining the company's efforts to the public. The business press was convinced that the tragic deaths meant certain death for the Tylenol brand as well, and that the incident greatly jeopardized the company. Forecasters were wrong on both counts. Had Burke made mistakes in his public handling of the problem, the blame would have been cast on him. He took that risk, as Quinlan did, because his sense of the right thing to do negated the risk of receiving personal blame for failure.

A second Tylenol incident isn't as well known but involved what may have been an even bolder risk decision. Tylenol had literally sneaked into the marketplace as a major brand of pain reliever. Marketed by McNeil Laboratories, a subsidiary of Johnson & Johnson, the Tylenol brand name became synonymous with nonaspirin pain reliever. Because McNeil was basically a pharmaceutical company that developed and sold prescription drugs to physicians, its management had neither the expertise nor the orientation to sell Tylenol through a mass media advertising campaign, as its aspirin-based competitors did. True to the McNeil orientation, Tylenol built its reputation through doctors' recommendations to patients who were allergic to aspirin or concerned about aspirin's side effects.

Tylenol sold at shelf prices substantially higher than those of aspirin products. Its pricing reflected the specialty market it evolved in, as well as the high profit margins that pharmaceutical companies need to support their R&D efforts to create new drugs. The combination of sales growth and attractive profit margins placed Tylenol in the corporate limelight.

As you might expect, this enviable market attracted competition. It came from Bristol-Myers, one of Johnson & Johnson's major rivals. Bristol-Myers launched its own nonaspirin product, called Datril, from one of its consumer marketing divisions. The product was offered at one-half the selling price of Tylenol, and the launch was supported by heavy consumer advertising. Tylenol had no advertising support at the time.

At this point, Jim Burke became personally involved in defining the Tylenol marketing strategy and, in particular, the strategy response to Datril. I was consulting for McNeil Laboratories at the time. The decision on appropriate action was difficult to make. Tylenol had strong support from the medical community; a strong case could be made that mass-market advertising would lose physicians' endorsements of the product. More important, market research showed that any penetration of Tylenol's brand position by Datril because of the lower price would have less impact on McNeil than the lost profits that would result from trying to match Datril's price.

Burke took the bold step of deciding to turn Tylenol into a legitimate consumer-driven brand. He restaffed the Tylenol organization with people from other areas of the company who understood consumer brand marketing. Then he immediately cut Tylenol's price to below Datril's. He began advertising, which cost the company dearly in short-term profits but eliminated a competitor and ensured that Tylenol would continue to be the brand identified by consumers as *the* nonaspirin pain reliever.

The strategy worked out well for Burke and his management team, but think of the consequences if it hadn't. A decision was taken that cost the company major profits in the short run and earned it a place in the Wall Street spotlight. If the longer term, positive results hadn't materialized, would Burke and his managers have survived to tell about it? Wouldn't it have been safer to stay with the high-priced strategy and blame any erosion on the business's competition?

As I said earlier, these are a few of the rare examples of successful risk management in the 1980s. Gambles that didn't pay off, however, were much more common. For example, Procter & Gamble (P&G) is a successful force in almost any market in which it competes. Much of this success can be attributed to its outstanding R&D capabilities; the company consistently creates breakthroughs that give it competitive superiority. For some reason, however, P&G's attempts to compete in the food industry haven't been nearly as lucrative. From my vantage point at Campbell, I had a chance to witness one of their misfires at close range.

The company decided in 1983 to enter the orange juice business as part of a move on the beverage industry. The decision made sense. Folger's Coffee was already a successful P&G product, and the company had recently purchased Crush soft drinks. Its attack on the orange juice market was a P&G classic; it relied on a breakthrough technology called "freeze concentration." The principle is simple: instead of concentrating products by adding heat and then removing the water by evaporating it, bring the product close to the freezing point and then remove the water. Since pure water freezes before sugar solutions do, careful manipulation of freezing point and water withdrawal can create the desired product concentrations. Campbell was working on such a technology at the same time, so we were aware of the process, its potential, and its pitfalls.

The advantage to this technology is that the juice retains a pure, fresh-squeezed flavor because no heat is applied to it. The disadvantage is the costliness of the concentration equipment. With an untested technology but an opportunity to achieve product superiority, P&G bought an orange processing company in Florida and launched the Citrus Hill brand of orange juice.

As intelligent as the senior management team was, they simply didn't understand the complexities of the business they were entering. They installed the appropriate equipment, entered test markets, and began a full-scale rollout. Their timing couldn't have been worse.

Because of the new technology, the company was committed to Florida as the single source of ingredients. Two of the worst freezes in history hit the state back to back as P&G began its rollout. Orange juice ingredient costs soared to prohibitive levels—an issue not factored into the equation by management. Using an available Brazilian source of ingredients, the company produced Citrus Hill as a blend of Brazilian traditional concentrate and ingredients from Florida freeze-concentrated sources. Whatever quality edge may have existed initially eventually became undetectable to even the most trained orange juice taster. Thus, the product failed to give the company the product superiority—and success—that it sought.

For a number of reasons, P&G lost focus in its core strategy as it tried to deal with the consequences of uncontrollable environmental conditions. We can only guess what its managers were thinking when they discovered that the supply of orange juice ingredients wouldn't be available to meet their market rollout commitment. They certainly must have thought about delaying the market launch. Backing off totally would have been a high-visibility risk compared to going with a mixture of superior and standard ingredients, hoping it would provide the key quality difference. Another option they had but apparently rejected was transferring their freeze concentration technology to processing facilities in Brazil; we can only speculate about why Proctor & Gamble didn't enter into a partnership with a Brazilian company. But it ended up choosing the same option almost any other company would have selected during the 1980s. It stuck with executing as much of the commitment as possible and only revised its strategies after failure actually materialized. Many P&G middle managers must have felt enormous pressure as they saw the strategy begin to fall apart but were unable to find anyone with the courage to call a halt to the company's commitment.

One aspect of successful risk management applies particularly to managers with high-risk responsibilities, such as managing a start-up or turnaround business. Such managers must be judged by how they manage the risks more than by the actual results. Delivery of bottom-line results must be evaluated over a much longer period of time than is typically allowed in most organizations for judging managerial performance. I know of no better way to destroy a promising but high-risk venture than to shoot down the project manager for not meeting the quantitative results expected in the short term. Yet such actions are typical of corporations with conservative management philosophies.

These examples should tempt you to revisit the treasury of your own company's failures. Look at what happened to the people involved and, if necessary, work to create an environment in which careers getting sidetracked because of failure is no longer tolerated. And protect yourself when participating in high-risk ventures by negotiating your own terms of involvement with your boss ahead of time, when your bargaining power is strongest. If you begin such negotiation after the project is well under way, you'll give out mixed signals about your commitment and will also seem to be insecure about your professional well-being.

Rule 4: Look Beyond Visible or Measurable Risks

This risk management area is undoubtedly the hardest for managers to change in a corporate culture. Yet if it can be done, it is one of the most fruitful development opportunities for a manager and well worth some extra attention.

We're all victims of our cultural norms; almost unconsciously, we filter information that doesn't fit the standard structures we've developed. Many corporate management processes are quantitative in nature. Although most senior managers think they're measuring what they manage, in fact, they're more often managing only what they can measure. That's how they get into trouble.

Any new venture or approach to an idea requires a sound commitment from those involved. But most people won't go out on a limb for a project that entails visible risk. They prefer to play it safe and stick to the corporate rules, even if they know the rules won't lead to a business success. Let me give you an example.

If there is one word that strikes terror in the heart of any food manufacturer it's *botulism,* a deadly bacteria that grows in products that haven't been fully cooked. Canned foods are particularly susceptible to it if underprocessed. Given the magnitude of the risk associated with botulism, it's not surprising that the U.S. food industry has developed strict procedures for monitoring and ensuring product safety for consumers.

Although fear of botulism is uppermost in the minds of food-processing technologists, certain foods have a natural immunity to the bacteria. If a food is acidic enough, the bacteria can't survive in it. Because fruit juices fall into this category, juice companies simply don't worry about botulism.

Following Campbell's purchase of Juice Bowl, there was an immediate clash between Campbell's botulism orientation and Juice Bowl's lack of concern about it. Processing methods at Juice Bowl didn't conform to Campbell's standards. If the Juice Bowl plant underprocessed some juice, as occasionally happened, it tasted sour. There was no health hazard in drinking it, but customers thought the product was spoiled. By establishing processing standards that tolerated the possibility of spoiled juice, Juice Bowl juice had a fresher, less-cooked taste. Campbell technologists admitted that their proposed change for safety's sake would degrade product quality; but just the thought of underprocessed product leaving the Campbell plant made them cringe. So Campbell's standards prevailed. I can't say the decision was wrong. The problem was in how the decision was reached. Instead of discussing the trade-off between product quality and the occasional sour samples, a set of standards based on conditions that didn't apply was implemented. The safest path to follow was sticking with the standards already in place.

The problem of managing only what we're able to measure isn't new. Good managers stay constantly alert to the possibility of falling into this trap. But that possibility is increasing as we emphasize information support systems and expect that our decisions can always be supported by fact-based analyses; we may stop looking as carefully at the decisions and job structures that are hard to quantify. Although some of these decisions may be critical for the business, it will become easier to either ignore them altogether or submerge them into other decision processes.

Risk is usually assessed with numbers as well as with less tangible factors. Almost every company says it looks past the numbers in its assessments of business strategy proposals, but don't believe it. The financial scorecard still holds great power, and the pressure on senior management to use this criterion is intensifying all the time. The Wall Street analysts, corporate raiders, and other financially oriented groups—ready to attack at the sight of the slightest bobble in a quarterly report—must all be appeased.

As a middle manager, you're caught between what you see as a potential light at the end of the tunnel and today's reality that you must give financial justifications for almost all of your actions. But don't lose faith. I've seen businesses become corporate stars when senior managers looked past the short-term numbers and stuck with their initial commitments. Perhaps the best example is Citicorp's Visa and Mastercard business. Today Citicorp is by far the largest and most successful bank for both cards. The company achieved this success because of its bold, risky strategy in marketing the cards back in the 1970s. More important, Citicorp stayed with its commitment even when early financial results were negative.

In the early days of bank-issued cards, they were almost exclusively issued by local banks to their best customers. The market was defined by the geographic area in which a bank operated. In the late 1970s a change occurred that created an opportunity only Citicorp recognized.

Bank of America converted its Bank Americard into Visa, which was operated as an association with national advertising support. Citicorp recognized this as an opportunity to solicit cardholders on a national basis under the Visa brand name. It introduced the practice of making direct-mail card solicitations to qualified households throughout the country. Citicorp did not have any significant information on the creditworthiness of customers solicited this way, since the method had never been tried before on a large-scale basis by any bank. But the company recognized that national marketing could earn it a position of market leadership. This risky strategy provided the account base Citicorp sought. Response rates to those solicitations in the late 1970s were nearly 10 times greater than credit card companies could expect today.

Unfortunately, its marketplace success created a financial problem for Citicorp in the early 1980s. Because credit approval criteria were only beginning to be developed for such solicitations, the early customers acquired by Citicorp had significantly higher credit losses than desirable. These bad credit risks, combined with extraordinarily high interest rates, caused Citicorp to absorb major losses from the card business. The numbers would have convinced many companies to withdraw or scale down. But Citicorp didn't manage the business by numbers alone. Its commitment to achieving national leadership in the credit card industry never wavered. Today its credit card business is one of Citicorp's largest and most profitable units, and it is often used as a model by the leaders of Citicorp's other emerging businesses in the risk management decisions they face.

It goes without saying that most managers try to do what's right for the business in executing their decision responsibilities. But what is right? What is the real impact of their decisions? How do they know when they've made a mistake?

Understanding risk management is even more important in an empowered culture, where all the rules have somehow shifted and decision-making power has moved to an entirely new level. What should employees do when they realize that the way they're being measured on job performance is applicable to only some of their responsibilities? What's easy to measure gets covered in evaluations, but entire areas are left out. One option is to ignore this question; accept the rules and perform according to whatever illogical performance standards are in place. This option is easy to rationalize. "Don't rock the boat because what they don't know won't hurt them" is compellingly safe logic.

The high-risk option is to do the right thing and try to accomplish all the objectives you've set, whether they're quantitatively measurable or not. Inevitably, this strategy reaches a point where the non-quantifiable factors lead to decisions that don't look good when only the quantitative factors are used in judgment. Now the real dilemma: in an empowered culture, it is assumed that the people closest to a job know best how it ought to be done; but spotting the need for change and executing it can put a manager out on a limb. If senior managers don't take the time to analyze the factors and discover that the measures, not your performance, are wrong, you might be out of a job. As I said, this is the high-risk option, but one you should take in an empowered culture.

In spite of today's new appreciation of empowerment, few managers take the risk of executing the right decision without the concurrence of senior management. As real gains are achieved by taking these risks, more people will be willing to challenge the system.

All middle managers need to better understand the dangers of managing only what they can measure. All businesses encounter the need to make decisions that can't be accurately measured.

When this happens, we tend to take the actions that minimize the chances of a visible and measurable mistake occurring. Errors that can't be accurately measured are treated as "theoretical"—meaning, they never end up on anyone's managerial report card. Unfortunately, these minimizing actions can cost an organization dearly in lost performance. A manager must understand and not be afraid of the unmeasurable risks involved in some decisions. He or she must also be aware of when subordinates are not taking certain actions because of the measurability issue.

I saw major flaws in Scott Paper Company's decision-making processes when I consulted there. Our study focused on Scott's process for deciding how to balance product demand and plant capacity. The conventional thinking in the paper industry was that excess production capacity creates financial disaster. This assumption was understandable considering that at the time a new paper machine cost more than a Boeing 747. Scott took the traditional approach: plant capacity was expanded only after new products proved to be successful. Then commitments were made to expand capacity to satisfy forecasted demand. Because of the lead time for ordering and installing new equipment, it wasn't uncommon for several years to elapse before the company was able to respond.

Our study evaluated the wisdom of Scott's strategy. We carefully examined the real cost to the company of excess production capacity and discovered it was considerably less than Scott managers thought. They had made the standard assumption that capital investments are highest whenever production capacity is expanded. But in an expansion of the entire system, the newer equipment would be fully utilized and idle capacity would be found only in the older, less efficient plants. So the economic problem created by excess capacity really wasn't as bad as initially thought.

More important were the costs we calculated of not having enough capacity. Scott had never tried to measure this side of the decision. Since the financial statement never reflected the lost profit opportunity, management ignored it; in fact, the lost profit was very real and quite large. Ignoring it caused Scott to miss additional market-share opportunities on new product rollouts, from which it never recovered.

We revealed to senior management the mistakes associated

with Scott's wait-and-see strategy in our consulting reports. They immediately made changes in their operating practices. When the final report was presented, one of Scott's senior managers turned to us and asked, "How could we have misunderstood these costs so badly?" Our response was quickly accepted. "Excess capacity was a constantly visible and financially measurable problem for you; the excess demand opportunity was not."

A similar situation at Diners Club involved the management of our collections operations. This is a labor-intensive and extremely important area. We had made major capital investments in the latest automated technologies to facilitate our collections effort. Some of the most expensive and sophisticated equipment we invested in were automated dialing systems that allowed our collectors to use more of their time being in telephone contact with our cardholders rather than deciding who to call and how to place the calls. We documented immediate productivity improvements. Our new system permitted each collector to handle twice the number of delinquent accounts, and the average time on the phone for each collector was nearly 25 percent lower than that of an independent collection agency. But we discovered a hitch in our system.

We weren't absolutely sure our new technology gave us everything, so we decided to check our performance against that of an independent agency. When we did, we discovered that the agency collected nearly twice as much money as our internal organization, and at a much faster rate. It seems that our dialing system recognized only one number to call as a contact point for delinquent accounts. The agency called neighbors and relatives. While we had greater success in utilizing our people, the agency was able to collect more money, which had a much greater impact on total profits. We knew how to measure the efficiency of our people, but not the potential dollars that might have been collected through a different system. We derived from the system the measure we could make accurately—staff efficiency—and ignored measures of effectiveness altogether because they were invisible.

Like Diners Club, most companies are so set in their cultural patterns that they don't realize the problems they're creating for themselves. Managers who constantly search for such situations and actively strive to correct them will be an asset to their companies. They will be the managers who recognize that achieving high visibility from taking on worthwhile risks and accounting for the measurability of both tangible and intangible factors are important elements of good risk management processes. Your ability to achieve positive visibility and expand standards for measuring risk can create benefits for many years to come.

Begin to capitalize on such opportunities now. Take an inventory of your job. Are the decision-making mechanisms too focused on quantitative measures? I'll give you a way to answer this question.

Ask yourself: if I could eliminate all performance measures used for my management responsibilities and I could make decisions based only on my experience and gut instinct, would any of my decisions be different? If the answer is yes, you could be overlooking the qualitative aspects of the decisions you make. If you have to pay too much attention to quantitative details, you're apt to ignore the qualitative factors that would cause your gut to arrive at different decisions.

Work continually to develop your skill at identifying decision processes that are inappropriately inhibited by quantitative standards. Start with your own area of responsibility. If you don't identify the qualitative dimensions of your area's responsibilities, there is little likelihood that anyone else will. Relying on numbers simply creates false confidence. Good managers will listen to someone who can make the case for using less tidy, but more meaningful, qualitative assessments.

As you build your skills, you're likely to spot more easily those cases in which overreliance on quantitative measurement led to inappropriate decisions. The decision to shut down a new product or venture is a classic example. The numbers will generally make an overwhelming case for shutting down and stemming the losses. Being given the opportunity to launch a new business or product is largely an act of faith. But when a company is under stress, acts of faith generally lose out to numbers arguments.

As a middle manager, you have a valuable perspective on business risk that your senior managers need to hear. Make your positions known, remembering that senior managers judge the risk factors in investment decisions by asking, "Do the people proposing the ideas have the confidence to sign up and go on the line to make their ideas a reality?" The answer to that question is often more important than any fancy numbers drill you go through in making your case. Throw in all the brilliant analysis and strategic intellectualization you want to; but if you aren't prepared to personalize the risks, the credibility of your work plummets. Remember this as you assess the role of risk management in your career.

Rule 5: Take Risks As If You Owned the Company

The best perspective for judging managerial risks is the ownership perspective. "If I owned the company, would I make this investment to grow the business or to improve its efficiency?" This vantage point can clear up a lot of ambiguity. Unfortunately, it's too often left out of risk management decisions.

Be careful when you're asked to play roles that force a non-ownership perspective on your decision-making. If you're given such an assignment, try to talk openly with a senior manager about your concerns and get them resolved before you get caught in the middle. Do it right at the beginning of the assignment so that no one gets confused about your motives.

If you take the ownership perspective in your decision-making, I predict that the resulting success in your job will bring you more and more assignments with a businesswide focus. You're also likely to be asked to participate in other projects with high risk-return ratios because such projects require a true ownership orientation. As this occurs, you'll be using your developing management skills alongside your people management skills because you'll need to manage the inevitable opposition from those people who don't have an ownership perspective.

You'll find that those who resist your initiatives are almost always seeking to define issues as narrowly as possible. For themselves they want well-defined performance measures that seldom change and that describe what they do, not what they contribute. They want to protect the status quo in the organization, and they try to force all decisions through the standard channels. Most important, they're terrified of the possibility of big change because they believe it threatens their function.

"Functionalists" have learned to fight off radical ideas with well-refined arguments. They have a winning record when decisions are made using traditional frameworks and staff approaches. After all, they represent corporate stability and believe in the value of progressing with small, steady, low-risk steps. The bonus is that there is no disruption of functional power bases.

As you refine your ownership perspective, you'll find that it prompts you to concentrate on investments that make sense to your customers. From an ownership perspective, customer purchases are the most important factor in the health of the business, including the final profits and returns to the owners. As employees, however, it's easy to lose this customer focus. Employees worry about how their actions are perceived—rather than about the business results of their actions—and about what role their functional area is to play in any decision. With an ownership perspective, you'll be less and less tolerant of efforts to protect processes and organizational structures that don't make much contribution to achieving marketplace successes.

Taking risks from an ownership perspective clashes with the concerns of the functionalists most visibly when business partnerships are attempted. If partnerships work, there can be significant wins for all players. But the risks of failure are very high, and usually not because the concept was flawed. Rather, failures occur because too many indirect attacks on the idea are made from within the partner organizations. These assaults aren't criticisms of the merits of the partnership but rather, ways of protecting the functionalists' territory. Without functional support, however, even good partnership strategies are much less likely to deliver bottom-line success.

So take heed if you find yourself in the middle of a partnership project that would bring about massive change in your company. The returns might be significant, but the risks will be greater than you first calculate. A partnership can breed invisible risks that sneak in from left field—as they did at Campbell when I was oblivious to the major risks involved with a strategy for licensing a new product.

Before the risks surfaced, those responsible for new product development in Campbell's Beverage Business Unit were ecstatic. Perhaps we had uncovered the perfect companion product to V-8: a juice marketed in Germany called Drink 10. Where V-8 is a blend of eight vegetable juices, Drink 10 blended ten fruit juices. Drink 10 had another unique twist: it was fortified to contain 100 percent of the recommended daily allowance (RDA) of ten essential vitamins and minerals. Research told us that consumers liked the product as a breakfast juice. Selling it in 10-ounce bottles was just one more opportunity to capitalize on the name. Our marketing staff saw the product positioned as Total cereal in liquid form. We knew it had a large sales potential if we could market it properly.

We went to the German manufacturer, arranged an exclusive license for the U.S. market, and began the process of refinement and field testing. That's when we crashed into a concrete wall thrown up by Campbell's government regulations staff. Was the product a food or a vitamin? You might ask, "Who cares?" but food and drug industry territories are powerfully protected—and kept separate—by the federal agencies that regulate them. We were up to our necks in red tape on the issues of possible vitamin overdose and toxicity—issues very familiar to the drug industry but scary terms totally foreign to a food manufacturer. The concrete wall of government regulation held firm and could not be overcome. We had to drop the effort. Perhaps if I had anticipated the opposition we would face, I could have better managed the partnership process and its risks up front.

At Swanson we used partnerships much more successfully. One reason might have been that we spelled out the partnership relationship as a key component to the business plan. Managers at many levels were involved from the beginning, and most of the risks were identified and dealt with before any partnerships were actually consummated. Our strategy was to give our product offerings microwave-compatible packaging and product design. As we gained momentum, we saw a real opportunity for a partnership with microwave oven manufacturers.

At the time, few major frozen-food companies had made any commitment in this direction, even though there were more than 40 brands of microwave ovens on the market. Our joint marketing programs with the manufacturers brought us many benefits: our products were used for appliance demonstrations, coupons for samples of our products were packed inside the ovens, and we had almost unlimited opportunities for coöperative advertising.

The partnership worked because we were open-minded about all the business opportunities and because we had the patience to gain a complete understanding of the business perspectives of our partners. Narrow and self-serving perspectives aren't compatible with risk management. When people ask, "What's in it for me?" or declare, "That's not a business area we're interested in," they're happy with the status quo, scared, or don't understand the potential benefits. Whatever the cause of their negative attitude toward high-risk partnerships, they create a real hole that its advocates have to dig out of. Successful partnerships are established when business leaders take a gamble, use foresight, and set the right tone. Then all employees go to work to make the partnership a success.

I had a completely different kind of encounter with a partnership risk that triggered an immediate battle over turf. Campbell was committed to expanding its position in the beverage market. We had developed our mission statement to focus on healthy and nutritious beverages. V-8 was the anchor point, and our purchase of Juice Bowl brought us a full line of fruit juice products. Our product development effort emphasized new child-oriented products that would be healthy alternatives to Hi-C and Hawaiian Punch. We were on a roll.

We never considered entering the soft-drink market, although the volume of those products was tremendous compared to that of our niche brands. In fact, our mission was to provide a healthy alternative to soft drinks. So I was somewhat surprised to receive a telephone call from one of the largest and most successful independent Pepsi bottlers.

He was worried. Consumers were becoming increasingly unhappy about only soft drinks being available in vending machines. Vending is one of the more profitable aspects of a bottler's distribution system, and consumer dissatisfaction was a legitimate threat to that profitability. Schools were the greatest area of concern, but the bottler saw similar dissatisfaction developing in health clubs and at other important vending sites. He had watched the healthy beverage strategy beginning to succeed for Campbell, as well as the rising popularity of the Minute Maid juice business, owned by Pepsi's competitor Coca-Cola. The question he put on the table was very simple: was there a way to develop a partnership in which the strong Pepsi bottler distribution system could become part of our juice product marketing strategy? He volunteered to present this idea to other Pepsi bottlers if we expressed interest.

I was excited about this idea as a business strategy, but hesitant because I knew what I'd face within Campbell. We had one of the largest and most professional grocery store sales forces in the country. The Pepsi relationship would strengthen Campbell's beverage business by providing broad-scale distribution in other channels such as vending. But it would weaken the effectiveness of the internal sales force because sales of grocery store beverages would have to be split between the Pepsi bottlers and the Campbell sales system. There wouldn't be enough volume to keep both sides happy. Did we support a marketplace business opportunity or an internal company asset?

The delicate discussions that followed took an exorbitant amount of time as legal documents passed back and forth. Meanwhile, the coalition of Pepsi bottlers was growing, signaling the great potential of the partnership. Then, unexpectedly, I was asked to head Campbell's U.S. soup business. When you win the lottery, you don't turn it down. I accepted. Unfortunately, the partnership discussions didn't survive the transition in the beverage business leadership. The new head of the business simply did not have the knowledge of and working relationship with the bottlers that I had developed. He also lacked the internal clout it had taken to defend the partnership idea against the efforts of a powerful executive who headed the sales force. As a result, we lost a tremendous opportunity to accelerate the growth of the beverage business.

The most important lesson in this example is that you can't go halfway in developing risky business strategies. Any time you jump from one half-realized opportunity to another, you're violating the ownership principle. No matter how appealing an offer might appear, always keep an owner's perspective on it: how would you respond to it if you actually owned the business?

I'm not telling you to pass up career advancement opportunities. But if you know up front that you can't make the commitment to fight for a risky business strategy and see it through to the end, don't even start on it. No one wins when you change course in midstream.

If you're in a high-risk, high-return battle, commit as an owner. Keep your focus on the fundamentals of business success—demand the best product for your customers, delivered in the most economical way. Make all other risk issues secondary; you cannot protect sacred cows in the company if a partnership with another company will get the job done better as far as customers are concerned. Almost all internal participants in the business strategy will have an asymmetrical view of the value of the partnership. They will want to see you use the partner a little but will expect to keep the advantages of partnership within the company. Without a strong internal advocate voicing a totally balanced perspective, the partnership won't be formed, either because the partner will become frustrated over issues of fairness and balance or because the benefits for both parties can't be realized.

If you do make the commitment and successfully form a partnership, you risk continuing battles with various internal people who will feel threatened by the new external players. Expect to see some ruthless games played; information may be distorted to make you look incompetent or biased. And you could be challenged about not working as a team player. But stick it out to the end. Your business won't be able to absorb a change in leadership if you hand the venture over to someone else. My Campbell experience with Pepsi is not a fluke. Although I turned the business over to a new leader, the failure to establish a partnership was viewed as mine. Ask senior management to allow you to see the venture through to its final stage before responsibilities are shifted.

Risk-Taking and Your Career

The pressure to invest in high-risk, high-return ventures won't diminish. Senior management will be looking for managers who can realize these visions. Get yourself ready for such an assignment so that when you're given it you can seize a tremendous opportunity to bypass your competition. But don't underestimate the challenge of getting all areas of your own organization to cooperate. Call on all your resources to make your case for change, and don't forget these five rules for honing your risk management skills.

Regardless of your company's level of awareness about risk management processes, you can and should be aggressive with your boss to ensure that you're judged by meaningful performance measures. Bottom-line results clearly have their place, but your control over these results is also important. I suggest you have these discussions well before results come in on your areas of managerial responsibility. If you don't, your credibility is in jeopardy. After the fact, you'll be seen as defensive in trying to rationalize bad news. If you want to be judged on the thoroughness of your process for managing uncertainties, you can't do it after the ball game has been played out.

Don't expect any change in the numbers focus given to most business decisions. Fact-based analyses will continue to dominate business. But not all business issues can be quantified, and you have a major opportunity to deliver real value to your company by forcing people to realize this. You might want to hang a sign over your desk to remind yourself to "measure what we manage, not manage what we can measure." You'll have to take the personal risk of pulling your associates out of the numbers comfort zone when important qualitative factors are missing from the spread-sheet analysis. It's not easy or popular to make judgments that can't be defended with numbers. Perhaps another risk proverb worth displaying is "I'd rather be approximately right than exactly wrong."

Finally, be sure to balance the risks to your career as you get involved in high-risk challenges. When you see a chance to be part of a high-risk activity with high-return potential, take it on if you can protect yourself by simultaneously working on projects that carry lower risk and contribute to steady career advancement for you. To do otherwise is like going to Las Vegas and betting your life savings on one spin of the roulette wheel. On the other hand, not putting some of your professional energies into an occasional high-risk gamble is like transforming all your earnings into savings bonds: you'll probably have a predictable but relatively boring career.

Start learning how to take on the risky challenges. Luck is the smallest factor in the risk management equation—playing smart will make you a winner in the long run.

7

Creating Your Career Strategy

I've always been amused when someone says to me, "Oh, this isn't a career, it's just a job." The way I figure it, whether you're delivering mail or heading a billion-dollar operation, most of your waking hours are spent at work. If you didn't actively seek out your job or you don't enjoy at least some part of it, you're probably a pretty miserable individual to be around.

We all invest too much time at work to go through life doing something that gives us a constant migraine. Most of you have considered to some degree what you plan to do for the next few years. I'm going to suggest that you make a strategic plan that can get you where you want to be.

Doing so isn't very different from creating a business plan for your company. Your company wouldn't consider moving forward without a strategic plan; neither should you abuse your career with sloppy management. Without a strategy, you place yourself in a completely reactive posture and your future will be controlled by events rather than by you.

Where Do You Want to Be in Ten Years?

When you begin to plan your strategy, think at least a decade into the future. It's crucial that you mentally get away from short-

166

term considerations. Looking at the next decade will force you not only to assess the role you want to play in the business environment but to consider exactly what that environment will be like.

During the late 1970s and early 1980s an army of AT&T managers were forced to experience some changes that dramatically affected all of their careers. The company knew there would be enormous change in its historic role as a regulated utilities giant. Managers desperately wanted to take the opportunity to unleash their talents in the computer industry. But they also wanted to retain the integrated telecommunication business. Something had to give, but no one knew what.

During this period of tremendous uncertainty, I had the opportunity to design and lead an advanced management training program for AT&T's fast-track middle management group. These managers had been earmarked by senior management as the best prospects for overseeing one of the company's operating companies for the next 10 years. So for four weeks, 40 hopefuls studied, ate, drank, and dreamed opportunity. As I listened to guest lecturers and to AT&T top management outlining great things for the company, I caught my first glimpse of the turmoil AT&T would face as it moved inexorably to its eventual breakup.

John DeButts, former AT&T chairman and CEO, delivered an address at the end of the program. His message was clear: AT&T was fully capable of competing in various markets. Doing so would reap unimaginable rewards, including the chance to bring new technology and new values into the utilities industry. DeButts was convinced that the culture and operating values that had built AT&T's core business should remain essentially intact. "The system is the solution" was the advertising slogan AT&T used far and wide, and it referred to much more than the company's particular technical systems. It was a statement of confidence about its culture as well.

To get things rolling, DeButts hired a marketing hotshot from IBM by the name of Arch McGill. Although the operating philosophies of the two men differed greatly, DeButts recognized McGill's successful leadership in the IBM culture and how valuable he could be to AT&T as the company tried to enter the computer market. McGill addressed the managers attending my management course and spelled out his vision of a customer-driven marketing focus, a message more radical than DeButts's. Such a focus was foreign to most of the company's managers. That's not to say they didn't like his blueprint for AT&T. They simply could not come to grips with its implications for the company.

The conflicting values of McGill and DeButts soon became evident. What AT&T managers liked and understood about McGill was his tie to the highly successful IBM. They could almost taste the glory he represented. But at the same time they yearned for the security created by the disciplined control AT&T exerted as a regulated monopoly. The problem was, the once clear image of AT&T and its operations grew fuzzy when these managers tried to bring into focus what the company would look like 10 years out. They saw big, they saw successful, but what vision was going to make it happen, and what did it mean for their careers? Most middle managers weren't sure, so they did the worst thing possible—they operated on a business-as-usual basis.

McGill's cachet as a successful IBMer just couldn't shake AT&T's traditional approach, and he didn't last long. The business press predictably documented the bloodbath the organization endured on the road to deregulation, and McGill and his ideas were not altogether surprising casualties.

AT&T's culture was shattered over a very short period of time. Hundreds of thousands of managers' worlds were simply turned upside down. The survivors were those able to identify and anticipate the changes and take action accordingly. In discussions I've since had with some of these managers, most indicated to me that they wished they'd taken Arch McGill's ideas more seriously in planning their own career responses. Of course, the fast-track status of these managers during the 1970s had disappeared by the 1980s. They still had blinders on when a freight train filled with change was coming straight at them. The message is clear: don't let that comfortable, snug environment you're in now seduce you into believing you're invulnerable to fundamental career-altering changes.

AT&T was drastically affected by a potent force for change in the 1980s—deregulation. Other forces, such as downsizing, will have a similar impact on companies in the 1990s.

Uncertainty Is Opportunity

Although the cultural changes now under way do threaten certain middle management functions, there's glory to be had if you're prepared to invest in a new career vision. New and diverse options are available to managers who aren't convinced that corporate life is the only assurance of a successful career. Other arenas may reap even greater rewards for managers willing to reevaluate their options.

The Independent Consultant

As companies trim their structures, they're more willing to engage consultants to supply services that used to be handled by internal departments. Functional needs still exist, but companies now want more options. They want to be able to change direction quickly, and that simply can't be accomplished when there are layers of specialized internal bureaucracy to get through. So they pay more for expertise in exchange for being able to control when and how they draw on it. As a result, consulting promises to become a major growth industry.

This new willingness to use consultants is far more pervasive than you might expect, and general management consultants are not the only ones in great demand. Companies now can and do rent managerial talent in many specialized fields; there are even some specialized CEOs who take turnaround assignments on a short-term contract basis. Does this scenario give you any ideas about where your career will be in 10 years? Will you be a corporate employee, or could you be a consultant?

Many managers who expected to find their pot of gold in the corporate environment tell me they got frustrated in their search. So they left the company, wrapped up their functional skills into a neat entrepreneurial package, and presented it to outside firms, including their past employer. The company doing the buying gets specialized skills without the overhead costs and added bureaucracy. Entrepreneurs doing the selling can be their own bosses by tailoring their skills to meet the needs of the marketplace.

A friend of mine recently sought my advice on leaving her job

at a large Midwest corporation to start up a communication consulting business. We sorted through her values and weighed
them against the benefits for her of working in a corporate environment. The balance was unsteady at best. She had done her
time and learned the ropes, but she had also grown tired of the
whole thing. Whereas corporate life inhibited her ability to make
a personal difference, on her own she could promote her own
values in a meaningful way.

Today consultants are popping up all over the place and in
areas that, 10 years ago, you'd have least expected to find them.
All kinds of consultants—financial, administrative, communication—are out there, and more important, they're competing globally. The New York financial whiz is trying to out-spread-sheet
the guy in Hong Kong. The administrative assistant who handled
relocation moves now has a global business facilitating international relocations for multinational companies. We're talking
marketable services of every conceivable shape, size, and texture.
What services can you offer corporate America—on your own
terms?

Staying with the Corporation

Although you might be tempted to focus most of your thoughts
on the possibility of starting up a small consulting business, don't
turn your back too quickly on corporate life. The large and successful company of the future will have unique opportunities to
play a more significant role in our society. Smaller businesses may
power the growth of the U.S. economy, but the large multinational corporation will dominate economic policy and global
trade agreements.

And there are many attractive corporate perks. In the past,
access to the corporate jet, black ties and escargot, and the instan-
taneous status of being identified with the company have been
important to some people, and they'll be important to some in the
future. More germane to this discussion is whether the corporate
environment is right for you. One thing's for certain: job retention is no longer guaranteed. And financial perks, even at the top,
won't necessarily exceed the monetary rewards of working in less
glamorous situations.

Be Clear About What You're Getting Into

The point is that you're going to encounter some complex trade-offs in deciding what you want and where you want to be. So be specific in your assessment. Taking into account today's changing management climate, clarify in your own mind what type of environment you want to grow in professionally. If you're thinking about starting your own business, remember that you're not merely leaving one job for another. You're reshaping some very basic aspects of the way you live and work. And for any career plan, identify where you *don't* want to be as accurately as you identify where you do want to be. An itemized list of what you want to avoid is a powerful instrument.

I've had to think about these issues many times in my career. On one occasion in particular, when I had decided to leave McKinsey & Co., the international management consulting firm, for the independent consulting life, I had no desire to build a large organization bursting at the seams with staff. Instead, I opted to work on a free-lance basis with the many corporations I'd worked with previously. I got the usual job offers, but I enjoyed the diversity of experience that consulting offered and the chance to develop relationships without being part of a large, problem-solving consulting team.

I remember quite clearly some of the immediate changes that hit as soon as I left McKinsey and started my venture. Minor matters to the corporate employee can have a great impact on the independent consultant—like holidays. For most employees, these are treasured days reserved for family outings and pure R&R. But I was out on my own working on a per diem basis—time off and holidays represented unbillable time. Every stroke of the clock suddenly held new, expensive meaning.

More important, after four years of free-lancing, I discovered that independence no longer meant liberty. I felt that my professional growth had stalled. My bank account was much fatter, but it wasn't enough. It rarely is. While I offered words of wisdom to various businesses, I felt too far removed from the intellectual stimulation you often get in organizations as a team member on the corporate payroll.

I had considered all the primary issues of being on my own; it was the secondary concerns, the things I didn't initially think held much importance, that got to me. It's like buying an expensive, quality car. Every nook and cranny and widget is a class act. The fact that the car is painted bright yellow seems unimportant, since the deal you've struck is superb. But by the fourth month, it begins to lose appeal and even seems to clash with the color of your house. Ultimately, you dump it for other symbols of success. "I want to be the boss, to run something," might not make sense anymore after some intensive self-assessment. The same realization often hits people who believed that making lots of money would lead to satisfaction and happiness. Be honest with yourself. It's your career, your life.

Put Your Vision in Writing

Thinking about your career strategy is great exercise, but thinking alone won't sharpen your vision. Ideas have a tendency to become soft, and thoughts can often be just fickle rationalizations for how you feel at a certain time. Unless you're able to articulate your strategy on paper, you probably aren't committed to it in the first place.

I've followed this practice for many years, and over time my vision of the future I want for myself has been considerably sharpened. My long-range objective is to return to a university and take a major role in the education of business leaders. Ideally, I'd like to create an educational environment for CEOs of major corporations. CEOs, particularly those just taking on that responsibility, would be brought together in a noncompetitive structure to share experiences and thoughts on strategic issues with retired CEOs and other leaders. The objective would be to accelerate positive change for the entire system and to encourage new leaders to make better decisions by learning from the experiences of CEOs from different industries.

Who knows if I'll be able to see this vision through to fruition. I do know, however, that my credibility as an educator is enhanced by my experience as a CEO working with the people who shape the larger corporate environment. The trade-off of acquiring more experience at Campbell to prepare me for my long-term professional goal versus accepting the challenge of turning around Diners Club was easy to itemize. Staying at Campbell would have given me a better chance to become CEO of a large public company (I was one of four identified contenders for the presidency). But Diners Club offered me business CEO responsibility immediately and a chance to see John Reed putting his stamp on Citicorp. (Reed became Citicorp chairman and CEO at age 45, six months before I joined the company.)

I took on the Diners Club challenge primarily because I believed the personal growth opportunities would move me closer to my long-range goal. Don't get me wrong. I wouldn't have made the decision to head up Diners Club if I didn't think I could meet the challenges it presented. But the swing vote was my vision. Compensation was way down on my list of considerations.

Your vision probably differs a great deal from mine. Perhaps you're thinking of starting your own business, joining a smaller firm, consulting, continuing your education, or following any number of career opportunities. Still, many elements of developing a career strategy are the same. Don't worry about home runs; until you assess some very basic issues, you'll never get out of the batter's box. Begin with an honest assessment of yourself. Examine your professional skills, your interests, and most important, your professional values. What roles and activities make you happiest during the time you dedicate to your job?

And absolutely don't make the fatal mistake of failing to evaluate the organizational environment before you land in one that is completely incompatible with your own professional style. If you are outgoing and aggressive with a passion for progressive thinking, you will struggle in a corporate culture governed by traditional values. You're kidding yourself if you believe that you can easily adjust to any environment, or that a six-figure compensation package guarantees professional bliss. Remember, the company certainly isn't going to change to meet your needs.

If you don't have a list of concerns that are important to you, make one. You might overlook some issues until it's too late to factor them into your decisions. When you are deciding whether to join a particular company, ask yourself if you would feel totally comfortable discussing the company and would describe your role there with pride and enthusiasm. If something about the company or the industry bothers you so much that you would rather avoid such discussions, I'd say you're not likely to fit in. When you're telling your peers how the organization makes decisions, how it motivates and rewards people, or how it supports career development, pay attention to the feelings that surface. Your embarrassment or enthusiasm in describing the organization are equally important reactions to recognize.

Tie Professional Decisions to Your Personal Life

Too few people link their professional decisions to their personal lives. It's absurd to believe they aren't related, but for many people the connection isn't recognized until there is conflict between the two.

I've forecasted some of the changes you can expect in the business climate of the 1990s, but what professional culture will be best suited to your personal values? You have options for how you position yourself for the changes expected to take place in the business world. Some will have a greater impact on your personal life than others. Determine whether the impact would be positive or negative, and how you'd manage both aspects of your life as a result. Don't ignore this.

Decide whether the business role you hope to assume complements your personal and professional priorities. What trade-offs are you willing to make on how and where you spend your time? How much control do you really want to have over your time?

For instance, I know several rising executives who struggle with long office hours and weeks spent away from home. Many have young children, and the tension created from trying to do the right thing for them can prove insurmountable. Dual careers in a household can also cause tension. Besides the expense of child care and manipulating schedules to make runs to the doctor's office, have you given thought to what would happen if one of you was transferred to another location, possibly to another country? This is the circumstance I've seen the most anxiety about, especially when it reaches the point of having to live apart, with one of you trying to make it home over the weekend.

Many of you might be contemplating how to increase your global marketability. Logically, you should seek an assignment in your company that provides more exposure to the international elements of your business. This undoubtedly makes a great deal of sense, but don't underestimate the impact on your personal life. A manager with no international experience who says, "No problem, I'm used to heavy travel schedules," has no concept of what "heavy" means. Domestic travel typically begins Monday and ends Friday. The international circuit, however, can keep you away for weeks at a time. More significant is the possibility of relocation abroad.

I know a manager with a highly successful career who'd never lived outside of the United States. He was offered and accepted a premier assignment as regional business coordinator in Asia, so he packed up his family and moved to Hong Kong. His 16-year-old son completely failed to make the adjustment. His wife didn't fare much better, and a year later he asked to be transferred back. Back home, he took a make-work assignment and never fully recovered.

If your attitude is, "I'll cross that bridge when I come to it," you're fooling yourself. Decisions such as these must be made before you plan your career strategy. Otherwise, the cost of reversing direction if you take off in the wrong one can be enormous, and satisfactory solutions are often impossible to achieve.

Take Small Steps as Well as Giant Leaps

I've seen few middle managers who know how to take the short-term steps required to enhance their chances for achieving longer term objectives. Our Diners Club middle managers are certainly no exception. During regular informal lunch sessions with this group, I try to discuss the broad career decisions they're facing. Inevitably, we discuss the possibility of either starting their own business or taking a senior role at a company substantially smaller than Diners Club. Many of them have thought about these options, but few have made plans for achieving such goals. Perhaps they just haven't been willing to talk with me about those plans, but I've pushed hard to try to facilitate programs for those who are serious about their aspirations.

For example, we've made a large resource commitment to collecting delinquent credit card payments. Some of this activity is handled in-house and some is farmed out to collections agencies working for us on contract terms. I've discussed with Diners Club managers the idea of building an independent collection unit within Diners Club that they could eventually spin off to service the company's needs as well as those of third parties.

Those claiming to be interested in taking an entrepreneurial direction believe they'd have a different perspective on their existing responsibilities if they had the chance to spin off a related business. Many of the managers are excited by the discussions about how this could be accomplished. But no one has come to me with a proposal to actually start doing it. I suspect that someone willing to take on the challenge will come forward eventually, but it's sad that it usually takes so long for people to grab this type of opportunity. I don't think Diners Club middle managers are atypical. Are you?

Getting Past "Go"

Once you've come up with a vision of where you want to be in 10 years, you need to start answering some critical questions. How do you plan to strengthen the skills necessary to accomplish your career goals? How will you maintain your credibility as you try to get the jobs you need along the way? Do you need to go back to school? Will a change of employer make sense at some point? Many answers to these questions are dictated by the five forces of change and the four key experiences. For instance, if you don't know the first thing about what it takes to build customer relationships, look for learning opportunities in your company and get involved. Additional education requires a time investment you might not be prepared to make right now, so perhaps you can broaden your skill base through involvement in other functional areas of the business. Just because your expertise is in finance or administration doesn't mean you're a permanent fixture there.

Don't overlook the non-work-related ways to move your career in the direction you want. If, for instance, you're serious about getting involved in international business, sharpen your language skills. You don't need permission to work at this.

The globalization of business has opened up new possibilities for managers from first- or second-generation American families. It wasn't long ago that these Americans tried hard to conceal their heritage, often even Anglicizing their names. But many maintain their family roots in their home countries.

I know at least one person who is aggressively exploiting his Japanese roots to establish business prospects for his company. Ironically, he can't speak the language and has only an indirect feel for some of the cultural barriers that Americans experience doing business with the Japanese. If he doesn't acquire more cultural knowledge of Japan—something most people think he already has—the advantage of having Japanese roots could actually become a liability.

If you plan to start your own business, you'll want to investigate the market area and the competition, perhaps using the services of an outside firm to conduct a trading area survey. If you want to further your education, don't enroll at an institution without checking into its credentials and finding out if it offers the training you'll need to complement your career goals. Always do your homework about new ventures that are part of carrying out your career strategy. It could save you wasted effort in the long run.

Don't bother writing down your career plan if you're not prepared to act on it. Try to answer all the questions I've outlined—and any others that occur to you—to help you figure out what you should do over the next year to move yourself forward.

Finally, don't leave your career plan stuffed in your inactive file, collecting dust. Review and update it at least once a year, just as a company conducting its annual strategic planning process would. What new information has changed your vision statement? How would you modify your strategies? It's not a good sign if nothing in your plan changes over the course of a year. Equally, there is probably something wrong with your plan if the fundamental vision doesn't remain intact from one year to the next.

Managing customer and people relationships, taking risks, and being a leader—these are the cardinal challenges of today's business environment. With a strategy built on these four key experiences, you can claim a real career win.

In the 1990s careers will be made, lost, or stalled in waves of opportunities. I can't emphasize too strongly how much opportunity there is for the manager willing to boldly take on the new challenges. Go after them—attack them with all the fury and passion you felt when you first entered the work force. Forge a career strategy that reflects the best of what you are—to be your calling card on the future.

8

How to Be Successful
Every Day

Now you have the key material with which to build a solid
foundation for your professional success. We've examined the
changing cultural rules you'll face over the next 10 years and
the key issues that must be covered in your personalized career
plan. And we reviewed the four basic managerial experiences
you'll need to develop. Now we're down to the nitty-gritty of
execution.

The actions you take every day on the job create the successes
that will open job options for you and advance your career plan.
If you don't manage the day-to-day transactions well, you simply
won't be given all the opportunities—or at least the right ones—
to succeed in your aspirations. Keeping your career strategy uppermost in your mind is absolutely essential when you're sorting
out your responses to these opportunities as they emerge. Still,
even the most carefully thought out strategy has no meaning
unless the choices that can move you along the desired path are
made available to you. Make no mistake about the importance of
managing your career on a daily basis.

In any profession, from sports to business, the difference between superstar and average performance is almost unmeasurable
in the short term. The accumulation of small, daily performance
successes over a long period separates the star from the under-
study. The superstar perched atop the corporate ladder didn't get

there because of one brilliant action. You've probably had an earful of words like *drive, dedication,* and *personal standards of excellence.* Clichés. And how about *hard work?* Another cliché. But clichés got to be what they are because of the truth in them. I'm not saying that hard work by itself is a magic wand. But unless you set your standards high and make the commitment to live up to them every day, not just once in a while, you'll be an average performer. And there's nothing wrong with that if you don't want to stand out.

Did You Earn Your Salary Today?

We've been hearing a lot about business ethics these days. One of the best ways to apply the issue to your own career is to answer the question, "How would what I'm doing look if it became a headline story in the *Wall Street Journal?"* I think that question could be used, with only a little rephrasing, to assess managerial performance: "How would I feel if my contributions today were the single basis on which my managerial performance was judged?" Can you leave work confident of being judged well for the performance contributions you've made today? If you were paid according to the results you deliver each day, would you earn the maximum you're worth every day? Remember, options for advancement will accrue largely because of your ability to distinguish your performance from the average performance of most others. Begin now to eliminate or substantially reduce the days you wouldn't want to use as measures of your job performance.

Most of us think of the compensation we get as something we receive annually or monthly. Wrong perspective, folks. All that perspective tells you is how much time you've punched in on the corporate time clock. Think about your next check as a fee you've charged your company for services rendered. If you aren't comfortable identifying and justifying the services you provided to get that check, you're operating on dangerous ground. Start preparing hypothetical bills itemizing your services for every paycheck you receive.

As you reassess your day-to-day performance, ask yourself if you honestly take the extra steps to add real value to the business, even when doing so involves going beyond your job description. Maybe you successfully completed your piece of a major project but only stood by and watched when the project failed to be implemented. No matter how well you execute your part, the business loses if the total effort fails. Never lose sight of this fact.

Contribute to the Bottom Line

During the 1980s, performance evaluations were usually based on individual efforts. Functional contributions were narrowly defined, and individuals were rewarded for their work by others with the same functional perspective. As we move into the 1990s, contributions that don't make a bottom-line, positive impact on the business are being increasingly discounted. The annihilation of entire departments or layers of management isn't happening because of any failures in individual performance but because of bottom-line issues. Functional areas that don't contribute simply won't survive the transition into the new culture.

It has always been wise for managers to keep an eye on the bottom-line contribution they're making. In the emerging value structure of the 1990s, this perspective will be even more essential. All your brilliant concepts, ideas, or accomplishments somehow become meaningless if they don't make a real difference to the business. I well remember the first time one of my ideas for an improvement wasn't fully implemented. It was to be my moment of glory, a success I could recall for years to come. I can still feel my initial high, as well as the ultimate disappointment.

During the summer following my junior year at college, I was lucky enough to land a job in a management candidate training program with Procter & Gamble at its Cincinnati headquarters. I spent time with other participants in a number of the company's manufacturing departments. There I familiarized myself with the operation. At the end of the tour, we were asked if we could suggest any changes that might be made to improve any part of the operation. No one at Procter & Gamble seemed to particularly expect any of us to "ring the bell" with a brilliant breakthrough. I personally felt obligated, however, to think up something monumental.

The summer wore on, and each rotational assignment intensified the pressure I was putting on myself to come up with a stupendous idea. Finally I thought I'd had a stroke of genius while working in the finished-product warehouse. All the company's brands were stored there before being shipped to customer locations. Aisles that seemed to stretch to infinity were packed with individual storage bays of finished product. Each bay was loaded from the center out with one particular brand of product. As each bay was cleared, a different brand almost immediately took its place. Because each brand and package size had a different case configuration, the bays didn't reach to quite the same point when they were refilled. A long, yellow line down each aisle designated exactly how far a bay could be filled.

As I wandered through the warehouse on a sweltering August afternoon, I noticed all the wasted space between the yellow line and the last case of product in each bay. Inspiration hit: was the best point at which to divide the two bays the exact center between the aisles? Having been trained in statistical methods as an undergraduate, I found a great deal of intellectual appeal in the question. I raced back to my desk and began calculating. Using the specific case size for all products and the specific dimensions of the storage bays, then factoring in the volume of inventory for different products, I discovered that indeed the dividing line should be shifted from midaisle. I calculated the extra space utilization that would result from shifting the dividing line, and with considerable relief I discovered that my idea substantially covered P&G's investment in me for the summer. I wrote up my report with recommendations and left Cincinnati with a satisfied ego.

I returned to P&G the following spring to participate in the company's full-time recruitment process. At the first break I had in my interview schedule I raced to the warehouse for a look at the results of my labor. The bubble burst—the dividing lines were still in the center of the bays. How could this be? When I asked why the change wasn't made, I realized I'd forgotten to include an important element in my equation. The cost of clearing out enough bays in a particular area to repaint the lines, or to have someone ready with a paintbrush every time one of the bays was emptied, wiped out any potential savings in my proposal. Bingo. It was a memorable experience in counting my chickens before they'd hatched.

Some business professionals get their moment of glory from coming up with a key idea that seems to solve a problem. The reality is that many strokes of genius don't work in practice. A good corporate leader understands that the only results that count are those that are successfully implemented. You should take the same bottom line perspective the next time you itemize your accomplishments.

Managers who work in big companies have become so used to seeing project work and staff activities get derailed before implementation that no one even gives it a second thought any more. The lack of implementation is partly the result of the increasing size and complexity of today's corporations. But the danger is great when we become accustomed to a slow pace of change and the expenditure of great quantities of staff work before implementation is accomplished; the ability to measure accomplishments by the bottom line is considerably impaired. All indications, however, beginning with the size and structure of businesses, suggest that the 1990s will witness a reversal in this situation. Apathy has no place in the emerging culture. Rekindle your energies to ensure your efforts are beneficial to your company's bottom line. Getting fired up begins with your attitude about success.

Components of Success

People often ask me if certain characteristics in middle managers are indicators of who will advance most rapidly. Obviously, numerous factors affect career success, but managers who find a way to deliver benefits to the business from their assigned responsibilities are always at the top of my list—like a Diners Club marketing manager who was put in charge of our revolving-credit product.

Revolving credit (activating a loan automatically by not paying credit card bills before the interest-free due date) is the most important feature of Visa and MasterCard, but Diners Club and American Express cards require payment of the balance upon receipt of the monthly bill. So income from revolving credit wasn't very important to our business, and marketing personnel assigned to this product generally operated as caretakers.

All that changed in the hands of this manager, who looked past "the way things have always been done." She utilized every scrap of market research information and data from our previous market experience to define new strategies that would fuel business growth. More important, she took ownership for each issue raised on any of the strategies and built tremendous support for her initiatives across every functional area of the company. An entirely new market for our company opened up because of her aggressiveness. She realized that most of our cardholders wanted a line of credit from Diners Club, but they didn't want it tied to payments of their credit card bills. Instead, they were interested in having access to an emergency credit line, using special checks we provided to them. Because of this insight from a marketing manager who refused to be just a product caretaker, we forged new relationships with our cardholders. The opportunity accelerated our business and increased this manager's visibility—the best type of win-win situation you can ever get.

Take Charge of Your Performance Review

The performance review will be the most important element in creating new options for your career growth. Be active in managing the way this process occurs. Tallying up your daily successes is a necessary base for successful evaluation, but it's not sufficient.

The performance review should be treated as an ongoing activity. Through feedback and change, it should enable you to strengthen specific skills and help your boss refine his or her perspective on your managerial qualifications. The process can work in a variety of ways. Through a method called "targeted performance management," NCR is taking steps to ensure that honest, ongoing communication about job performance occurs between managers and employees; at the same time, the company is trying to eliminate the disparities of fact or perception that can exist between them. Employees' specific job functions are grouped into key areas of responsibility called key result areas (KRAs). So that manager and employee will each know exactly what the other expects up front, result expectations and measurement methods are defined in writing. In addition, employees are measured on *how* they do a job, as well as on *what* they accomplish.

A worksheet outlines concrete examples of the employee's job performance and aspects of it that could be improved. Both the manager and employee review this information, on which the formal annual evaluation is based. Properly executed, the review process holds no surprises—there is no ambiguity about whether employees met the results expectations. They know exactly how they'll be measured, and the manager has the flexibility to make goal changes as the year progresses.

As part of your performance evaluation, express your desire to acquire skills in any vital areas where your boss sees performance deficiencies. Be sure you're getting the truth on this assessment. Many managers are unwilling to talk frankly about their subordinates' weaknesses. This reticence isn't doing you any favors, so it's to your advantage to initiate an honest discussion about your weaknesses. Sometimes you need to be creative to get such information out of people who don't want to confront you face to face. I know one manager whose direct reports had to get the real news from his administrative assistant. It might not be right to have to go to this amount of trouble, but obtaining the truth is more important than how you do it.

Once you and your boss have identified and agreed on your areas of weakness, get specific and positive: what specific behaviors would change your boss's opinion? Your goal is to gain joint commitments that will allow you to improve your skills and show that you are overcoming your weaknesses.

Any performance review is only as good as the people who execute it. Before you go into your next review session, do some serious planning about the assessments and changes you want to see happening. Many people get too focused on the performance rating as the key factor to be managed during the review. The rating is, of course, important, but it's only one element in achieving your goal—namely, the acceleration of your career strategy. So start asking some vital questions. What are realistic career development options or new job assignments that will propel you down your desired career path? Let your boss know that you have specific preferences in career advancement options should they become available. What positive things does your boss have to say about your skills and qualifications to take on such responsibilities? How are you evaluated in areas critical to your next career options? What will it take to prove your skills in areas with deficiencies? Now you have begun to identify the gaps in your skills that need to be closed, as well as the objectives of the review process, from your own perspective.

I can testify from many experiences with performance review discussions that putting performance weaknesses on the table and discussing them honestly is one of the most constructive career development steps you can take. As a manager, one of the most positive outcomes is having an employee prove you wrong about his or her capabilities. Whether it's the advertising manager who wants to prove his expertise in marketing or the manager trying to overcome her people management deficiencies, a focus on the problem and on performance objectives gets everyone thinking more clearly about what's really important.

Be Prepared to Move Sideways—Even Backwards

For managers who are serious about making their career strategies a reality, short-term lateral or even backward moves should be acceptable pieces of the strategy. It's psychologically difficult for most of us to believe that making a move everyone else views as a step backward could actually be a way to set up a long-term win, but I've seen it work on several occasions.

The proposal to make a lateral or backward move almost never comes from the person involved. It usually originates from your boss during a discussion about your career path. It's too bad that more middle managers don't think of taking these lateral or backward steps. If you initiate the proposal yourself, I think your boss would make an even greater commitment to protect you through this career development step. Whenever I've been a party to such a move, I've always intensified my efforts to ensure that nothing goes wrong. The business has an obligation to make good on its end of career development negotiations.

Take on Special Assignments

Seek your boss's approval to take on projects, however risky, whose business results are broader than your job description charter. But think carefully about which projects you'd like to do before you talk with your boss. Such a project could be related to performance skills you want to improve, or it might be an opportunity to help make a cultural transition in the organization. Just make sure that you gain ownership of whatever expanded responsibilities you take on and that how you carry them out will be evaluated in your performance reviews. As you make these commitments to take on expanded assignments, obtain commitments from your company to support your personal development program. If you handle it correctly, it's unlikely you'll be turned down on self-development projects that involve your broader commitment to work for the good of the business.

Many middle managers miss real opportunities to get win-win results for the business and themselves through creative handling of special assignments. Undertaking a project to satisfy course requirements in a degree program is a classic example. For some reason, employees taking courses are often reluctant to approach senior managers about such a possibility. That's a mistake. We've had outstanding business benefits at Diners Club from using employees' course assignments to analyze activities in new functional areas. Not only have we benefited, but employees have usually gotten high grades on such projects because they're based on real business situations.

An acquaintance of mine who worked for a brewery in Mexico found some creative opportunities within his company to fulfill his course requirements. As a public relations activity, the brewery conducted tours at its main plant, which had a beer garden where people could relax and socialize following the tour. My friend was taking a market research course toward his MBA degree, and he asked company executives if he could use the beer garden to collect product research data. They supported the concept, and the idea quickly expanded; the beer garden became a permanent source of data for new-product market research. My friend was put in charge of the venture and eventually achieved significant business gains—going far beyond the mere fulfillment of his educational requirements.

Be aggressive in managing job performance issues. Preparing for the review session by defining your agenda items is essential. Equally critical is how you follow up. Depending on how well you get along with your boss, ask if you can write a memo summarizing key discussion points and conclusions. It will allow you to shape the tone of the discussion so as to benefit your objectives. But even if your boss prefers being the one to write the memo, use it to review your progress the next time you get together for a performance review. Between reviews, document the activities you've undertaken and the results you've achieved that address issues critical to your performance. If you're doing a good job of managing your daily activities, you should have little trouble documenting your performance for the follow-up evaluation.

A final piece of advice: hold performance review sessions as frequently as possible. Many companies would just as soon wait a year or longer. Some don't have formal reviews at all. For them, the closest thing to a performance review is a passing comment from your boss like, "You're doing a great job. Keep up the good work." Then the big surprise: your rating or salary increase doesn't reflect the "great job" you're doing.

If your company's review process doesn't permit frequent discussions, initiate informal reviews with your boss. Try to establish a quarterly lunch to discuss your performance. By doing so, you'll be letting your own ideas about your accomplishments and shortfalls, rather than your boss's expectations, set the agenda. More frequent reviews also allow you to set more specific targets and expectations. Be aware, however, that you'll be going on the line with your performance results more visibly. You'll be served up the good, the bad, and the ugly all at the same time. But I think it's worth the risk.

The Art of Networking

Networking is as old as our corporate heritage. Politicking, "kissing up," sharing ideas, exchanging secrets—whatever you call it

and whatever your opinion of the age-old art of collaborating, it's still an important activity for career growth, especially with associates in your own organization. Many people equate the management network with corporate politics. Well, maybe they're partially correct. But networking is not a matter of getting plugged into your company's rumor mill; that's an unproductive waste of time and energy. Networking is the creation of a managerial network that you can use to enhance your career options.

Keep in Touch with Those Leaving the Company

Professional support groups are essential to any manager's success. If you handle networking well, you'll be establishing resources you can call upon later. If you've had people management assignments, stay in touch with the people who have worked for you and keep tabs on the top performers.

Conduct exit interviews with as many of your direct reports as possible, as well as with anyone further down in the organization who shows great potential. In these interviews, learn what employees thought was good and bad about their career and the time spent in your organization. The feedback is extremely valuable to your effort to fine-tune the management development processes in your organization. You will also benefit from having created an ongoing connection. Learning about ex-employees' career expectations in their new jobs will give you an opening so that you can periodically get back in touch to see how things are working out.

Maintaining contact takes relatively little time, but it can pay enormous benefits. You should build a flock of disciples who would be ready to return to your organization for the right job and the right opportunity as you move through your managerial career. Your good people are a major resource you can tap at some time in the future. Don't minimize the value of such disciples—or the liability of not having them.

Depending on the breadth of your people management responsibilities, you might want to create a formal tracking system for your personal use. Keep data on the strengths and weaknesses of your subordinates, their career aspirations, and their assessments of their career experiences after they leave your area. Knowing people's special needs and staying updated on what's happening with them will pay off when you make the call requesting that one of them join your team. It takes relatively little time, but it does take discipline to make a tracking system into a management asset. It's worth the effort.

If you're not familiar with some of the new PC-based software available for tracking managerial relationships, you ought to look into it. The new software is a far cry from a name-and-address book. It allows you to keep detailed information on each individual, to do quick updates on the information, and to sort your files in just about any way you want. This technology can multiply the benefits of networking if you take a little time to actively update and maintain your records.

Reach Out to Your Peers

Be equally aggressive in networking with your peers. You should look upon your involvement in company training sessions and conferences as not only a chance to learn and exchange information but as a vehicle for peer networking. Every manager who has succeeded in changing an organization has had the support of his or her senior manager and peers. You need these networks not only to be successful but for feedback on the appropriateness of your change recommendations.

Citicorp is an organization that always recognized the value of network relationships among its employees. Indeed, face-to-face meetings are often held—at considerable travel and facilities expense—to give employees informal access to individuals from other parts of the company. A valuable publication distributed to all employees attending these off-site meetings is a directory of the attendees, complete with picture, career background, and current address, fax, and phone information. Citicorp employees know how to maximize networks through these sessions.

Even if your company doesn't facilitate networking to this extent, you will have natural opportunities to take the initiative. Don't overlook volunteering for responsibilities such as chairing the United Way drive or other community or company activities. Such activities can quickly build your network into an effective asset.

Allocate time for the ongoing cultivation of peer contacts within your organization. Don't necessarily take the next plane back after a meeting at corporate headquarters. Investing an extra hour in an informal update with someone from a sister organization can pay unknown dividends at some time in the future. You'll create allies you can call on when you need support for controversial proposals down the road.

You should even consider helping people beyond the call—this will create IOUs for future needs you may have. The process is informal, but I guarantee it's a winner. The IOU worked for me at one point when an employee we traded to a sister company simply didn't work out and was terminated within six months of his arrival there. Although we had no obligation to do so, I decided to help pay for his severance package and outplacement costs. Several years later we needed help from that organization's senior management. We got it immediately, with benefits to us far greater than the cost of the financial investment we had made in one employee's severance package. I have no doubt that their quick and positive response was related to our initiative in the earlier transaction.

Find and Use Mentors

A mentor is the ultimate supporter, a guidance counselor, and a sounding board. Many companies have documented the value of informal relationships between senior managers and middle managers as a catalyst to the careers of the latter. I've had several key mentors myself, and there is no question in my mind about their positive impact on my career growth.

Mentor relationships can help in unusual and unforeseen ways. One of my mentors was Dick Kovacevich, a Citicorp senior executive. When I joined the company, Dick was my boss's boss; he was responsible for the international segment of the consumer banking group. During my first year I had several opportunities to bring Dick up to date on Diners Club's business status. I think he was especially sensitive to the challenges I was facing, since he'd built his own Citicorp reputation by turning around the New York consumer bank. Over some long dinners, Dick offered insightful counsel and, more important, gave me reassurance at a time when my doubts about Diners Club becoming successful were beginning to engulf me.

The real value of my relationship with Dick became apparent during a major reorganization of Citicorp in 1985. Rumors about "something big about to happen" raced through the company days before any formal announcement was made. It was a big change, all right, and Dick was smack in the middle of it. For a year, he and Rick Braddock had shared the responsibility for the consumer banking business as a result of John Reed's elevation to chairman. Everyone knew that Reed would eventually announce whether Kovacevich or Braddock would run the consumer bank. Braddock won the prize. But there was more.

Divisions were also restructured and my area was shuffled into a new credit card business. In one fell swoop I was to change bosses and inherit a new second-level boss. I'll never forget the call I got from Dick at 9:00 A.M. on the day of the big announcement. He told me in advance about what was happening and about his own change of responsibilities. Even as he faced turbulence in his immediate area, Dick still reached down in his organization to reassure me that things would be okay. He offered good advice that helped me personally and the Diners Club business get through the transition. You can't establish this type of mentor relationship by randomly choosing someone to play the role.

Unfortunately, mentor relationships usually don't work when an organization tries to formalize them. These relationships work because of the chemistry between the two people involved. Mentoring is a two-way street, but you can find a mentor by initiating potential relationships.

Remember, chemistry can't be defined by rules. What makes mentoring work are trust, respect, and experience. Initiate contact, but never try to force a relationship. And never choose a mentor because of an individual's status or ability to promote you. Such motives violate what this relationship is about and are usually blatantly clear to the object of your misguided attentions. Actually, in many ways the best mentor is often someone outside your organization.

Using Networks

Network relationships, whether at the mentor, peer, or subordinate level, all have similar managerial value. They are of critical help whenever you go through a period of managerial stress, a condition no one can avoid. At those times, talk about your concerns with people you trust and use them as a sounding board. Don't become an island separated from the rest of the organization. If becoming isolated is your reaction to stress, it's too late to build your network. On the other hand, actively building networks every day takes relatively little time.

I remember watching a very good, recently hired senior executive in one company completely self-destruct because he didn't have a network of managers to help him through tough periods. It wasn't obvious who was to blame for his having no network, but there was no question that it was missing and that the lack of it caused his resignation.

This senior manager had been hired to create a new global business for the corporation. To staff the effort, he called on the human resources group to help identify talent from within the company. All he got was damaged merchandise. The capabilities of the people referred to him for the new venture were exaggerated, and he naively hired some of this questionable skill for his organization—with inevitably disastrous results. Burned by the internal process and feeling shut off from the rest of the corporate network, he turned exclusively to outside hires for all his key positions.

Perhaps he assumed that he'd be able to accomplish his mission using the newly recruited talent, and that the networking issues could be resolved after his initial business success. But it didn't work out that way. With communication increasingly cut off, little problems surfaced that could have been fixed by managers who knew the ropes. But his organization became an island with no support from the parent company. Then a major crisis arose. It became apparent that other areas of the company had resources that could make a difference to this venture, but the people in charge of those resources weren't about to hand them over as long as this senior manager was in charge.

You didn't need a fortune-teller to predict the events that followed. With no internal network, and with his business in trouble, he was left hanging. Everyone recognized that his departure, which was cordial enough, had little to do with his actual accomplishments but was the result of a bad corporate fit—effectively, his lack of access to the corporate network. Be careful that someone doesn't write a similar story about you.

Bottom-Line Realities

Many studies have profiled fast-track middle managers in corporations and identified the key factors in their advancement into senior-level positions. Their profiles are very similar. In one study done several years ago by Citicorp, the conclusion was that three factors made the greatest difference in obtaining senior management status: depth of experience, success in meeting important management challenges, and utilizing mentors.

I don't believe the broad factors will change significantly as we progress further into the decade. But I do think that some of the specifics of these factors will change to reflect today's culture. In particular, I feel managerial results will be increasingly judged by bottom-line contribution to the business. I also believe performance reviews will become considerably more important and will be conducted far more professionally. Finally, I think the managerial value of networks will be recognized at all levels of the business, but particularly at the peer and subordinate levels, reflecting the full implications of flat organizations and empowered cultures.

As you intensify day-to-day management activities along these lines, you'll be recognized as a valued resource to your organization. However, your focus on daily accomplishments will require enormous effort and energy with no guarantees for success. As part of your plan, decide for yourself how big a commitment you're prepared to make.

When new opportunities begin to surface because of your

efforts, they will create some of the most interesting but difficult choices of your career regarding changing jobs and companies. How will you respond? The answer must blend the personal elements of your career strategy with the specifics of the opportunities. In the final chapter, this issue is brought into focus.

9

Advice on Tough
Career Decisions

There's no tougher career decision than deciding whether to
change jobs. Most of you have been through it at least once—
enduring sweaty palms and sleepless nights as you try to evaluate
the trade-off of the known versus the unknown. Is now the time
to try something new, and is this opportunity the best one? Sure,
there's plenty of reason to worry—your livelihood is at stake. But
while you risk making a mistake, you also have a great opportunity to accelerate your career.

I wish I could give you absolute rules on how to make a job
change decision, but you are the only one who can weigh the
priorities and values you've incorporated into your career plan
against the daily accomplishments and frustrations generated by
your current job environment. What you need most are questions
to help you make an informed decision.

Assessing What You Have in Hand

Before you even consider leaving your current position, create
your personal report card. Analyze your job from two perspectives: what you have brought to the job, and what it has brought
you. More important than assessing your accomplishments in the
job is thinking about your future in it. If you were to spend more

time in the job, what else could you accomplish that would go on your performance record and what could you gain from it as part of your self-development program? You know a lot more about the potential continuing benefits of your current job than you can ever forecast about a new opportunity. Do your homework before making a final decision.

Should you decide to call it quits, try to time your departure to coincide with a big win. Naturally, this isn't always possible, but if you're working on a project that could set the business on its heels, complete it. It's far better to leave a job as a winner than as a mediocre performer, or worse.

Keep in mind, however, that job changes that occur too quickly, often early in a manager's career, neither help the organization accomplish its goals nor allow the manager to round out his or her managerial skills. I've adhered to the following general rules on timing job changes for most of my career. If my energies are absolutely focused on bringing an important change to fruition, there's nothing that will persuade me to abandon the effort and switch jobs. In these periods I've handled recruiting calls with a firm "Thanks for considering me, but I don't want to explore the opportunity now since I'm trying to make my mark by meeting an important challenge in my current job." Believe me, recruiters understand and respect this attitude.

I've taken a similar stand on internal promotions. If internal opportunities don't arise at the time you'd like them to, you can enhance your credibility and market value by walking away from them. I faced this choice early in my days with Campbell Soup. As the company's new vice president of marketing for the Swanson frozen-food business, I got off to a fast start by using the emerging microwave oven as the catalyst for making wholesale changes in the business. I received a lot of visibility, and success led to an exploratory lunch with the executive heading the soup business. I was flattered by his offer of leading the marketing organization for the soup division, but I turned it down because I had unfinished business with the Swanson line. Not once have I regretted my decision.

Ironically, I was later convinced to leave my Swanson post for a transitional role to general manager for all Campbell Europe business. This assignment went exceedingly well but, as it turned out, consisted of only six months studying the European food industry. I never had time to leave a permanent mark because a major Campbell reorganization opened up a very senior domestic assignment for me before I'd even relocated to Europe. In retrospect, maybe I should have held back one more time and used those six months to drive the frozen-food venture one step higher.

Always remember that your professional credentials will depend almost exclusively on what you did with the positions you held, not on how many there were. Make sure you aim for the right objectives in building those qualifications.

Evaluating Internal Promotions

Suppose there is a promotion opportunity you're considering within your company. How should you size up this option? There are several key factors that you need to consider to reach the best decision. Begin with the fundamentals of the proposed job.

First, determine what you must do to be successful in the job, and assess your own abilities. What challenges in the assignment will senior management use to judge your performance? When you are absolutely clear on how success will be measured, assess how confident you are that you can meet the performance standards. The last thing you want to do is take on an assignment that could create a black mark on your record. If you believe senior management is unrealistic in its expectations or that it's not prepared to invest sufficient resources to achieve the goals, pass up the promotion. You've got to believe you can be successful in a job before you take it.

I remember the plum job that once hit the posting board at Campbell Soup. Normally, candidates with the credentials would have been falling all over each other to get in line for interviews. But the informal communication network worked well: no one applied for the job. It was well known that it had been created because the corporate president literally forced one of his senior managers to do so. That senior manager—to whom the unlucky new hire would report—made no bones about his view that the job was a waste of time. Winning the job would have been suicide, so not surprisingly, it was filled by an unsuspecting outsider. He lasted less than a year.

Second, evaluate the assignment's contribution to your self-development program. How would it stretch your skills and give you usable new capabilities? Would it prepare you for the management culture your corporation is developing? Most important, would it further your long-term career strategy?

If the job involves a relocation or a major change in your work style, don't ignore the impact on your personal life. What changes would you be forced to make in your personal life, and do you have the time and energy to make those changes? Your career plan document will help keep you from overlooking any crucial aspects of your life that would be affected by such changes.

Third, assess your fit with the new people in the organization—your new manager, your peer group, and the people reporting to you. Gather information from your own observations and discussions as well as from your network contacts. If you hope to leave the mark of your style and philosophy on the organization, you can't ignore the compatibility issue.

Although your ability to gather and evaluate the facts about an internal job change is far greater than it would be for an external opportunity, you can still depend on being surprised—more often unpleasantly than pleasantly. As a result, I can't overemphasize the importance of being extremely comfortable with your reasons for accepting a position before you trade off the advantages of spending a longer time in your current job.

It's certainly tempting to totally trust your senior manager's motivations and wisdom when you're offered a promotion. Sometimes that trust is justified, but often accepting the job would not be in your best interest. If you don't do your homework about the job, the company can't be criticized for having made the offer. Don't believe that you will be blackballed if you turn the offer down. I've seen few companies penalize someone who rejected a promotion but who made it very clear why.

Scouting New Turf

There's probably no greater gamble than changing companies. You're not just changing jobs, you're moving to an entirely new and different environment. There's something to be said for the comfortable familiarity of the company you've been with for a while. But there are sometimes tremendous opportunities to be gained by leaving.

Say you have stable managerial relationships and your job performance is consistently good; you have no pressing need to make a job change. But your career development seems blocked by a dearth of internal options, and there are no clear routes upward. What should you do? First, ask yourself all the same questions I suggested that you ask yourself about an internal job opportunity. The factors in both kinds of decision are practically identical. The difference is that the risk-return ratio is much higher for an outside job change. So you must be sure about what you want from a job change, and absolutely sure that you can't get it inside your own company.

If you decide that you need to change jobs, don't sell yourself short or cheap. Whatever can go wrong when exploring internal options increases exponentially when you're looking into external opportunities. Don't take a job that wouldn't bring you big gains in your self-development program. Compensation and job title are certainly important, but your career strategy should always come first.

Keep in mind that career barriers can be caused by frequent company changes for small gains, as reflected in the thousands of middle management résumés circulating throughout corporate America. Many unemployed managers made three or more company moves over a 7- to 12-year management career. Each change increased the risk that they would fail to land the next new job. Most executives won't even look at individuals with this kind of history; they are viewed as job-hoppers who probably can't work successfully on any company's management team—a perception that spells certain death for a career. Don't be enticed into moving to a new company for marginal gains.

Before you begin to explore an outside job opportunity, be very clear on what you are doing and why. The process is in your hands, even when the initial inquiry is a cold call from a head-hunter. The decision is still yours whether to close off discussion with the caller or to initiate the first stage of exploration.

If you are actively soliciting opportunities to make a job

change, others will find it reasonable to assume that you've thought through the full career implications of this action. Evidence from executive search and outplacement firms, however, suggests otherwise. If you believe you can maintain total confidence throughout the process, wake up. And if you are presented with an offer, don't expect the new company to give you a month in which to reach a decision—they will want a firm decision in a matter of days. You must know what you plan to do *before* you pursue external opportunities, and you must make firm and speedy decisions.

Fully analyze all the issues before you decide to leave your company. If you see a career crisis looming if you stay, examine what is going wrong before you decide to leave. Study the total situation carefully and objectively. Perhaps some of the problems point to a reexamination of your career strategy. If you've had a hard time dealing with your direct reports, maybe people management isn't your strong suit. If you've resisted adding financial savvy to your administrative capabilities, maybe you're in the wrong line of work. Decide what you want out of your ideal next job, then define the approach you should take to get it.

If you are forced into an outside search because you've lost your job, you have less control over your options. The fact is that any potential employer will look more favorably at a candidate who has a job than at one who doesn't. Furthermore, there is the issue of your financial situation. A good rule of thumb is that landing a comparable job takes approximately one month for every $10,000 in salary. There's nothing worse than having to compromise your expectations about the ideal job to satisfy income needs.

Get It Straight

Let's say that you're involved in serious discussions with a potential new company, and that you carefully explored and assessed senior management's expectations about job performance, your ability to meet those expectations, and the fit between the job and your career strategy. You've made a good start, but there are other important areas that are often overlooked and that require your attention during a job interview.

Try to uncover why the company is going outside its organization to fill the position. Some reasons are legitimate, but others should set off sirens. Probe beneath the initial explanation for the facts to back it up. For example, if you're told that the position is available because the company's growth rate is outstripping its ability to promote internal talent, do some checking. You should be able to quickly determine if the company is really growing fast. If it isn't, you should be very suspicious. Try to uncover more information; make sure that the real reason there are no internal candidates is not that it's perceived as a dead-end job, or that the boss is disliked.

Companies also look outside to fill a job that is so high-risk that none of the qualified internal people will take it. Obviously, you won't be told this directly. Perhaps you can get to the bottom of the situation by getting the names and backgrounds of the internal people being considered and finding out why they think they aren't appropriate for the job. Another explanation you might hear is that the job requires skills different from those typically developed in-house. You had better look realistically at your promotion possibilities in so specialized a job.

Also ask questions about turnover patterns in the area you would be responsible for, as well as about companywide turnover. Turnover is related to a company's track record on internal promotions. Be concerned if your interviewer isn't willing to give you specific information. Needing to maintain confidentiality certainly wouldn't explain such reticence. You'll know the situation soon enough if you join the company, so you have the right to the information prior to your decision.

Size Up the Environment

It's smart to get information on the managerial track record of your potential new boss. Your own observations are important, and you can gain tremendous insight by carefully preparing questions for your interviews. You want to find out exactly how this manager's basic management philosophies support or oppose your own. Without this knowledge, you won't be able to judge whether the environment will allow you to achieve your career goals. If the company is truly interested in you, everyone involved is likely to be on his or her best behavior during the courtship, telling you just what you want to hear. But it is to no one's advantage if carefully censored communication masks problems that ultimately surface after you've made a commitment. If you're working through an executive search firm, very often it can provide objective information about the company and its culture. With their reputations on the line, placement firms aren't anxious to place someone who doesn't work out any more than you want to be that someone.

Obviously, some information is going to be difficult to get. You'll need to be on your toes during interviews; use all your senses to capture relevant information every time you have a recruiting contact. If you get into the company's facility, pick up clues about what's going on by observing the people and bulletin boards you pass in the hallways. Ask questions. Although learning everything you can about a job before you make your final decision can be tough, it's essential if you expect to make the best choice when the job is offered. As one inventory check on the company, review the four audit tests provided on the four key experiences. See if you can answer enough of the questions to define the company's culture. Analyze whether the areas of traditional leaning create any problems for you.

If you decide to accept the offer, I caution you to resist the temptation to equate a fast start in your new job with achieving an immediate win in an assignment. The six-month honeymoon on any new job is a common phenomenon. You're new, you're there, and you want to be noticed. You have a list of ideas that you're certain can greatly benefit the business, bringing you recognition for your efforts at the same time. But don't try to be a 90-day miracle worker. Wait, watch, listen, look, touch, and feel. Understand that after the honeymoon, the organization will inevitably test your real capabilities.

Your ability to get support to make and execute fundamental change will only occur after you've passed this test. A common error that fast-track managers make is to believe their initial successes during the honeymoon phase are permanent accomplishments. They're ready to move on to the next challenge before they've developed the skills needed to pass the company's test, and before they've established their credibility as potential leaders in the business.

Evaluate the Rites of Passage

One final element shouldn't be overlooked in evaluating a potential new employer. What are the rites of passage into the executive suite? Almost every corporation establishes certain crucial capabilities that managers must exhibit before they're considered qualified for senior management roles. Usually these skills aren't explicitly written down, but you can identify them from careful analysis and observation. Perhaps presentation skills are important, or a keen knowledge of the global market, or even the ability to develop a business strategy. Again, executive search firms can help define a company's expectations.

An example of such a requirement is Citicorp's insistence that all its senior line managers have superior analytical skills with which they can explain business performance. The corporation gives its business managers a great deal of responsibility and freedom, but there are monthly tests of these managers' skills through the reporting and review process. All business managers must explain detailed financial and operating information on the performance of their units. Senior management confidence in its managers and its willingness to support their business initiatives are based on their performances in these monthly reporting sessions. If they don't have the analytical know-how and presentation skill it takes to regularly pass this test, their advancement is definitely capped.

Consultants Beware

There are numerous factors to consider in deciding if a job is right for you, but how well you'd fit into the company culture in the long run is as important as any of them. I've seen many people take a job with a perfect cultural fit who subsequently had difficulty getting promoted. Nothing was available because they were specialists in the organization.

I've watched this happen time and again as consultants from consulting firms try to make the transition to corporate management careers. A classic career strategy for high-performing MBAs from the major business schools is to take a position at a prestigious consulting firm, which serves as a postgraduate finishing school for their business education. Indeed, the strategy makes a great deal of sense; consulting assignments can expose you to senior management thinking in a variety of industries.

To successfully execute this career strategy, you move up through the ranks of the consulting firm by demonstrating an ability to quickly define strategic actions to solve client needs. You are also able to persuade clients to take your recommended courses of action. Consulting rates are so high that clients usually will not take on such expenses unless they have a problem of pressing strategic importance. By the same token, they won't consider a consultant's study a success unless it outlines a definitive plan for change.

Although a consultant's work does provide intellectual stimulation and wonderful opportunities to learn, a consultant's job isn't directly transferrable to a corporate management role. More specifically, the consulting world's steady diet of obstacles to strategic change doesn't reflect reality inside a corporation. Such megaissues arise periodically, but no one could survive in a corporation expecting a steady round of that type of work.

The transition from consulting to corporate management is extremely tricky. Making the wrong choice of organization or role can be disastrous. Many consultants make the career change after a successful experience with one of their clients. A senior manager becomes impressed with the consultant's skills, a job opportunity exists in the organization, the consultant is ready for the corporate management challenge, and the courtship turns to marriage. Often, a consultant's first job in a corporation is a high-level strategic staff position that exploits the background and skills he or she acquired in the consulting world.

The big career question is, what happens after the transitional assignment? If all goes well, the consultant quickly adapts to the role of corporate manager. He or she will provide good results on key business matters, develop a reputation in the organization for quality work, and make the transition from a staff role into a line management position. Many times the line assignment is a revenue-oriented job, such as marketing manager. From there, the former consultant's continued success leads directly to general management.

But some consultants never make the transition because they focus all their energies on the big picture. Over time they lose credibility, become bored, and leave by mutual agreement.

There's another snag consultants can hit when entering the corporate world. Some corporations operate their internal businesses much like consulting firms. These corporations tend to be fast-paced and aggressive and are constantly searching for new ideas that will bring better business results. Since ideas are critical in this kind of culture, the most powerful managers are those who demonstrate they have the best ideas. The same avenue to power and success exists in consulting organizations.

A consultant entering this kind of corporation sometimes finds the transition to the corporate world to be relatively easy. But not always, especially after the honeymoon is over. New managers quickly run up against internal competitiveness, which creates what has been called "management power from sharp elbows and a quick mouth." These organizations are highly political. Power-mongers, anxious to generate streams of successful ideas to their credit, cause dissatisfaction among many new employees. High turnover is often the result. In fact, such corporations often encourage turnover to generate even more fresh ideas. When someone leaves, the corporation just recruits another aggressive consultant.

This operating philosophy can work from the corporation's point of view, but there are many casualties among consultants who enter these environments to become managers. They appear to have failed in the transition from consulting to the corporate world when, in fact, they failed at judging how well they were going to fit the organization they joined.

Options for Retooling Your Career

Instead of moving to a new job inside or outside of your organization, maybe you're contemplating the idea of taking time off from

your career for full-time professional development or career re-
tooling. The most obvious example is the decision to return to a
university for an MBA degree.

In my opinion, an executive MBA program that allows you to
continue in your job while pursuing a degree during the evenings
and weekends is the way to go. I recognize that my advice doesn't
conform to current practice: many people decide to return to a
full-time MBA program three to five years after getting a bache-
lor's degree. But I think an advanced business degree program
should be designed to complement ongoing work experience. I'm
not an advocate of going from one work experience to full-time
study at a business school, then on to a new work experience with
the MBA union card. I've seen the failure of too many MBAs who
return to the work force with bundles of newfound but inappli-
cable insight.

A poignant situation that occurs with some frequency is the
40-year-old manager who got off track. The so-called midlife
crisis of people in their early forties is well documented, and
forces contributing to it certainly won't diminish over the next
decade. This crisis will strike more and more middle managers
who see the shrinking opportunities in their professional lives. In
the past midlife crises occurred even when job environments
were stable and promising. That simply won't hold true in the
1990s as the early waves of baby boomers reach the critical psy-
chological point in their lives at the same time that they experience the stresses of derailed careers. Many will make major
mistakes in their decisions about personal transitions and career
issues. The best advice is to keep your career on track in the first
place—an intention that, admittedly, can't be realized all the
time.

The logical options for recasting your career from the midst of
a midlife crisis aren't so obvious. I would recommend that you
maintain an ongoing personal development program to parallel
your career development. It could be either an academic or a
community-focused set of activities that complement the specific
strategies you're pursuing through your job. Corporations have
become much more enlightened about the importance of sharing
their managerial talent on issues of community interest.

Broadening your managerial contacts and perspectives is another benefit of pursuing a parallel career development program outside of your job. It will extend your network beyond your employment base. Consider starting a parallel career development program, regardless of your age. If you do, I don't think you're apt to face a crisis when you feel the time has come to make a change. The parallel career gives a broader base to your career options and enables you to capitalize on your total experience. A friend of mine, for instance, turned his love of wilderness camping into a lucrative business.

A few individuals have painlessly made the transition into second careers. We've all seen the stories about people like the senior advertising exec who threw in the towel and opened a ski lodge somewhere in Vermont. There's a good chance that making such a change will become less the exception and more the rule of smart career management in the 1990s.

Although some opportunities may become overbooked as baby boomers capitalize more and more on their hobbies and other interests, there are still possibilities. Maybe you'll start a moonlighting consulting business to test the waters and your skills. If your family has roots in the emerging Eastern European countries, you could incorporate your knowledge of your country of origin into your present position, or find a new position related to that country. Use your frequent-flyer points to take a working vacation there to explore the business territory. Be aggressive—the field will soon become crowded with players whose skills are equal or superior to your own.

Putting It All Together

As you distill the material I've given you in this book, I hope one core message stands out: if you're serious about your professional growth over the next decade, you can't escape the need to think about where the management environment is headed and what it means to you. Shape your strategy around the general corporate trends I've identified, and go to work right away on building your own four key experiences.

As you take advantage of the new opportunities, recognize that most of them will arise out of your success today. Ask yourself

every day whether your efforts are delivering the performance everyone—your customers, your direct reports, your peers, your boss—expects of you. Are you delivering them? Examine your responsibilities in the broadest possible context, then go beyond the expectations of your boss or senior management.

I was brought back to the reality of how people expected me to perform at Diners Club shortly after I joined the company. One Sunday afternoon my wife and young daughter toured our executive offices. As I busied myself gathering papers, I was struck by the infinite wisdom of the six-year-old when my daughter remarked that her dad was obviously doing a great job for the company—he worked hard to keep the bathrooms clean. Bull's-eye. Obviously a child would consider clean bathrooms an important aspect of overall business performance, perhaps even more relevant to success than net worth. But how many others watching Diners Club's progress during the turnaround period felt that clean bathrooms were a better sign of success than financial ratios? Probably a lot more of them than I was willing to admit.

All of us consider parts of our jobs not very important to our overall performance. But some people judge us solely on these seemingly irrelevant areas. Don't overlook clean bathrooms as you attempt to produce the results that will eventually create your career development opportunities.

Your career success is determined by no more and no less than your current job performance. If you left your organization today, what would be your legacy? Business and financial results, you might answer. But these accomplishments are only temporary. Your real legacy is in the processes you've created to ensure that the success you've achieved will endure after you leave.

You can solve a hunger problem in the short term by giving food to starving people. Or you can solve the problem permanently by teaching people how to farm. The management equivalent is the decision-making process. Don't try to be an overnight success, but reach for the future by developing skills and strategies that contribute to your long-term performance.

Good luck to you as you strive to enhance your career through this decade and into the new century. I hope you are successful in delivering the results in your current job that will give you the career edge you're seeking as you pursue your long-term career aspirations. Finally, I hope you leave your mark in ways that are shaped, to some extent, by the ideas I've given you. If so, I will have accomplished my own objective of leaving a mark on the 1990s landscape by helping a group of managers not only avoid potential crises but emerge from the challenge as winners, both personally and professionally.

Index